The Van Cliburn Legend

The
Van Cliburn
Legend

by Abram Chasins
with Villa Stiles

Doubleday & Company, Inc., Garden City, New York

1959

Library of Congress Catalog Card Number 59–8260

Copyright © 1959 by Abram Chasins and Villa Stiles
All Rights Reserved
Printed in the United States of America

Contents

5

Foreword

It never hurts, I suppose, to begin at the beginning, and this book really started with a letter to my collaborator:

September 2, 1958

Dear Villa:

Constance and I had dinner with Van last night at a quiet little Italian restaurant in the East Sixties. When I broached the subject of doing a book about him, he looked wide-eyed, stretched his huge hands across his chest, and said with an embarrassed little laugh, "But, Abram, there isn't a book in *me*."

I said I knew this; that a "biography" of a man barely twenty-four was not quite what I had in mind. But perhaps there *was* a book that would point to the many vital implications of the Cliburn legend, satisfy the public's enormous curiosity about him and his background, and seek to correct current misapprehensions: one that might illustrate the political, artistic, and social overtones of the phenomenon, illumine the place and problems of art and artists in our society, demonstrate how much or how little the mechanisms

7

of management and publicity can manipulate public acceptance. And finally, I added that such a book might further a sharper awareness and understanding and appreciation of our national cultural resources. "Oh," he said, "that's different. Maybe all that could accomplish something constructive."

Am seeing Van again tonight. He's working like a fiend, although suffering terribly from a tooth abscess, operated on yesterday. But the night before, in spite of all the pain, he practiced from midnight to 7 A.M. How do you like our boy?

Best,
Abram

From the outset, our desire to tell this story as fully and accurately as possible led us to many people who have been both sympathetic and helpful and to whom we wish to express deep appreciation.

Our first thanks are due to Nola and Theodore Rhodes, whose closeness to the Cliburns enabled us to authenticate many doubtful points, whose enthusiasm for this project encouraged us constantly, and who have given generously of their time and effort.

We have also benefited by numerous other kindnesses: Lyde and Charles Devall of the *Kilgore* [Texas] *News Herald*, Hazel and Allen W. Spicer, Mme. Rosina Lhevinne, Mrs. Edgar Leventritt, Rosalie Leventritt Berner, Schuyler Chapin, and Skitch Henderson related vivid memories to us; Gleason Frye, the Reverend Richard R. Hamilton, Frederick Steinway, Gil Gallagher, Ellen Karelsen Solender, Joyce Flissler, Harriet Wingreen, and Sue Bachner Rothman contributed keen observations and reminiscences; Natalie

Marcin read proofs and Thomas Lask read considerable portions of this book in typescript and made typically pertinent suggestions; Sidney Fields unselfishly gave us valuable sidelights gathered in the course of articles on Cliburn for *Guideposts* and the *New York Mirror;* and Dorée Smedley supplied moral assistance from the beginning.

We are further indebted to William Judd and to the Elizabeth Winston organization for courtesies far beyond professional co-operation: for permitting us the liberal use of office documents, reviews, photos, tour itineraries, and programs; to William Schuman and Mark Schubart for a delightful luncheon and an enlightening session at the Juilliard School, where they are, respectively, president and dean, and where Sheila Keats also aided us materially. And we value the unusual devotion and authority Miriam Molin has brought to the formation of the index.

I personally want to express appreciation to Lester Markel of *The New York Times,* Max Ascoli of *The Reporter,* and Arnold Gingrich of *Esquire* for their editorial invitations which first set me to assembling Cliburniana and for their permission to utilize some of the material originally printed by them; and to Elliott M. Sanger, executive vice-president of WQXR, whose idea of presenting Cliburn's now-historic concerts over that station provided not only a public service but also the opportunity to observe the pianist under singular circumstances.

To my wife, Constance Keene, I am under the deepest obligation, for it was she who alerted me to Van Cliburn and who finally suggested that I tidy up my articles, notes, recollections, and experiences and organize them into a book. I fear, however, that she has felt many moments of regret over that suggestion as she found herself taking on

Foreword

one duty after another, personal and professional, to enable me and Villa Stiles to get on with our work. We both thank her.

ABRAM CHASINS

New York City
December 31, 1958

The Van Cliburn Legend

1
The 13th of April
in '58

The overseas operator in New York assured Moscow that she was still struggling to put the call through. "Keep trying, *please*," she pleaded for the fiftieth time with the central operator at Kilgore, Texas. "Keep trying until the line is free. He wants to talk to his mother."

The whole world, it seemed, wanted to talk to his mother. First it had been the call from New York. "Hello, Mrs. Cliburn? This is CBS calling. We want to be the first to congratulate you."

"Is it official?" Mrs. Cliburn asked tremulously, wanting to make sure it was not just another of the two days' rumors. Final and confirmed, Columbia Broadcasting assured her with the voice of authority. Would she care to speak to her son if their correspondent could arrange it?

Speak to Van, in *Russia?* Tears sprang to her eyes. Still—
the Sunday evening service at their church was due to com-
mence in a very short time, she explained to CBS, and if
she and Mr. Cliburn didn't leave the house soon, they would
be sure to be late. CBS understood. Lines were held open
while someone wrote down the telephone number of the
First Baptist Church in Kilgore, Texas, where Moscow
could reach the Cliburns at prayers——

However, just before they left the house the call came
through. Tightly Mrs. Cliburn pressed the receiver to her
ear. "Is that you, Van?" she called.

Over the long wastes of ocean, over the curve of the earth,
came the far, thin voice: "Mother, are you there? . . . They
gave me first prize!"

"I know, dear, I know," she answered, her voice tense
with emotion.

"You know?" Van asked in surprise. "How? Has anybody
heard about this?"

Had anybody heard! She started laughing.

Later that evening as the church service closed the minister held up his hand to detain his congregation. "I don't
usually do this sort of thing," he announced, "but if I don't
tell you this, you're going to hate me. Van Cliburn has won
first prize at the International Tchaikovsky Competition in
Moscow, and it's going to be shown on television tonight."

About the only people in Texas who weren't glued to their
TV sets that night were Mr. and Mrs. Cliburn. They didn't
have a chance. By the time they reached home the Dallas
papers were already on the job. The phone never let up—it
shrilled like a banshee.

The next day when they awoke they found their small
home in a state of total siege. Photographers' bulbs popped

off around it like balloons at a circus; neighbors and sight-seers began to arrive by the minute, to block the street with cars; telegrams piled up so fast there was hardly time to read them; the yard, the walk, the sidewalk in front were teeming with people.

Everyone had heard.

And yet, less than a week before, not one American in ten thousand had ever heard of Van Cliburn, despite the fact that in his own country and at the age of nineteen he had already won an artistic recognition at least comparable to the Soviet award that catapulted him to unprecedented celebrity.

When the news flashed across the Atlantic pandemonium and consternation broke out in newsrooms all over the country. No pictures, no background material, little or nothing in the morgues, hardly anything anywhere on the tall young man who had "conquered Russia" and in a split second had become a central object of excitement and curiosity to 175,000,000 fellow citizens.

The big wire services and syndicates, caught unprepared, were suddenly seized with the same inspiration: call his home-town paper! Those who got through to Winston Gardner, editor of the *Kilgore News Herald*, found a harassed man robbed of his usual unruffled calm, nailed to the phone and struggling to get his own paper to press. While he fed answers to *Newsweek* via long-distance about the local boy who made good, a man from *Time* was perched on the desk making furious notes. Finally, after the latter had scoured the town for more succulent copy, Gardner bid him good-by with a wry, fraternal smile:

"So they want to put him on the cover," he sympathized. "Now, how they going to do that? You've got to get something juicy on a subject to make a good cover story, and what could anybody find like that on *Van?*"

The headline hunters weren't the only hungry ones. On two occasions out-of-town conductors of considerable renown startled me out of a sound sleep, phoning in the middle of the night to ask if I would intercede with Van to appear with their orchestras as soon as he returned. Sleepily, I told them that the line was forming on the left. . . .

And all this was only the beginning. United States correspondents were keeping the wires red-hot with the latest Cold War sensation from Russia. Telephotos showed Van being publicly embraced by Nikita Khrushchev; Mrs. Khrushchev had sent him flowers; admirers had asked him to play special encores. Russia's sovereign musicians paid him homage. The streets and hotels and concert halls were thronged wherever he appeared: Moscow, Leningrad, Minsk, Kiev, Riga.

Meantime, back in blasé New York, the capital of celebrities, all those who had ever known the winner—actually anyone and everyone who had merely laid eyes on him— were badgered in their homes, cornered in their offices, pestered on the telephone, and begged almost tearfully to fill in some of the missing details.

The hullabaloo found Mayor Robert F. Wagner just as excited as the rest of the world. "This is a wonderful thing, that boy's winning the Russian prize," he said. "We ought to give him a great reception here."

So exactly thirty-one years after the golden young Viking Lindbergh rode up Broadway in the first great ticker-tape parade, the blond young Texan Cliburn found himself atop the back seat of a convertible, waving his enormous hands unbelievingly at an ever changing horde of human faces that laughed, cried, and shouted hysterically.

"Bravo, Van, bravo!"

"Atta boy, Texas, you sure showed them Reds!"

"Van, you're the greatest!"

"Well done, boy!"

"Go get a haircut!"

The bands blared. The children sang. Officials made speeches. Nothing like this had ever happened before in American history. A musician—an artist—was a national hero.

At his first concerts the public battled for admission, the critics strained at their adjectives. Similar great receptions awaited him in Philadelphia and Washington.

Again Van crossed the Atlantic to appear in London, Paris, and Amsterdam, where his name on the marquee initiated box-office riots. At Brussels he represented the United States as soloist with the Philadelphia Orchestra under Eugene Ormandy to chalk up another sensational triumph. Back again for a tour of our outdoor amphitheaters, public enthusiasm rose to rapture as his drawing power smashed every previous record. From the Hollywood Bowl to the Lewisohn Stadium—no pianist ever before drew so many people. Every seat filled and thousands swarming over adjoining rooftops at a dollar a throw or backed up five deep before the railed gates to catch an occasional phrase wafted on a benevolent breeze.

His fame spread like a brush fire, enveloping everyone— the young and old, the musical and nonmusical alike. Two visiting Texans up North for the sights, circling the island of Manhattan on a sightseeing boat, were enchanted to hear their guide sing out: "See that building over there near the

green dome? That's where Van Cliburn went to school."
He was pointing out the Juilliard School of Music.

Yes, everybody now knew the name of Van Cliburn. He
had been on TV, had been on the radio, had been held up
to the public in blazing headlines; thousands of stories and
hundreds of huge pictures splashed over the front pages. Everyone everywhere knew all about him.

And yet——

Just after WQXR, the radio network of *The New York
Times,* had finished broadcasting a concert of Van's from
Boston one Sunday afternoon, the telephone rang. A nice
lady asked, "I wonder if you could tell me what Van Cliburn's first name is . . . Yes, his *first* name, please. No one
seems to know it!"

So it appears there *is* something more to be told about
Cliburn. One wishes that the answers to the boundless questions being asked were all that easy. They aren't.

To begin with, Dear Lady, his first name is Van. But not
really. His entire name is Harvey Lavan Cliburn, Jr., although from the day he was born on July 12, 1934, in
Shreveport, Louisiana, no one has ever called him anything
but Van.

2

Trumpets Offstage

The name Van Cliburn stuck in my mind nearly ten years before it became a part of the language. I first heard it one soft spring evening in 1949 when I went out to La Guardia Airport to meet my wife, pianist Constance Keene, on her return from a three-month concert tour.

"American Airlines flight 184 now arriving from Dallas at gate three" was echoing from the terminal loudspeaker just as I arrived. The blurred words put me in a mood of gay anticipation. I always looked forward to those long taxi rides home, for they provided us the chance for uninterrupted gabfests, a luxury hard to come by once we were caught up in the daily routine.

After the porter put the bags into the cab and we started off, I settled back with the question, "Well, how did it all go?"

"All right—pretty much as usual," Constance answered, and filled me in briefly on the highlights of the trip. Suddenly she leaned forward. "Oh yes," she said brightly. "I *did* run into something unusual I've been waiting to tell you about. After my recital in Henderson, Texas, a striking woman came backstage with her boy. She was so warm and dynamic and made so many intelligent comments about the music that I asked her who she was and what she did.

" 'I'm Mrs. Cliburn,' she told me. 'I teach piano in Kilgore, and this is my son, Van. He wants to be a concert pianist.' "

"What's so unusual about that?" I asked, remembering my own touring days. One prodigy per town, paraded before the visiting artist by an overzealous parent or teacher, is par for the concert course.

"Well, wait till you hear," Constance continued. "What struck me about these people was that they never mentioned a word about how good the boy was or what he had done—simply that he was working hard and hoped someday to live in New York and go on with his studies. They were driving right back to Kilgore that night, and of course I had to leave on a sleeper, so I couldn't hear him play.

"But all over Texas, wherever I went, I was asked over and over again, 'Did you get to hear young Van Cliburn? We're right proud of that boy.' And here's the real bombshell— I finally discovered that last year he won the Texas State Prize for piano, which carried an appearance with the Houston Symphony under Ernest Hoffman, and then some contest that entitled him to play in Carnegie Hall, as part of the National Music Festival. But not a word of all this, mind you, from either the mother or the boy."

I admitted that this certainly was a switch. Usually, the boastful claims thrown out about such youngsters turn out to be preposterous when the home-town genius finally plays for the visiting celebrity. Rare is the experience that does not, in some way, wind up as an embarrassing exhibition, even when the unfortunate child is genuinely gifted. My memory plunged back to the time I heard a famous prodigy of the twenties. Her father burst unannounced into my studio at the Curtis Institute one day, literally dragging the bewildered tot at his heels. Shoving my student off the piano bench, he swept the little girl up in his arms, plumped her down, and commanded: "Play! Go on, play! Show Mr. Chasins how a genius can play." My heart went out to the pathetic wee creature, who was much more interested in the doll Papa had just snatched out of her clasp. But play she did, spectacularly and brainlessly, with fantastic facility. When she finished, her father started the name-slinging: "Hofmann, Backhaus, Zimbalist, Sembrich, Stokowski . . . they all say she's the greatest genius they ever heard!" Perhaps she was—but this great talent later repudiated the keyboard and her avaricious father and all the torments they represented.

Constance cut into my thoughts with, "And he's such a charming boy, too, with beautiful manners! If he's half as good as they say he is we'll be hearing from Van Cliburn."

My memory filed the name. . . .

Two years later my wife found herself booked to play in Kilgore at the high school auditorium. Sure enough, among the backstage visitors afterward were Mrs. Cliburn and her son. "By now I'd begun to think," Constance told me later, "that there wasn't any Mr. Cliburn. But I was wrong. After the auditorium went dark and we left the building together there he was waiting outside." This was her first introduction to Harvey Lavan Cliburn, Sr., purchasing agent for one of the local oil companies. The head of the family was a most sensitive person, bespectacled, soft-spoken, and gentle.

For some time they all stood there, discussing Van's future and the possibility of his obtaining a scholarship at Juilliard the following fall. This, at the time, Constance remembers, seemed to be the family's uppermost ambition. And evidently that particular moment stands out in the mind of Cliburn senior as one of special significance to his son's early career, for he has often since said, with emotion in his voice, "If we only had a picture of the four of us—us three and Connie—on the high school steps that night in Kilgore!"

Van came into our lives again in 1952, the year Constance and I both served on the jury for the Chopin Scholarship, a one-thousand-dollar-for-study award offered by the Kosciuszko Foundation of New York. The contest is held in an old brownstone mansion. The piano is located at the far end of a beautifully paneled drawing room, full of paintings of Polish poets and patriots. The contestants must pass the judges' tables on the way to the instrument. Constance was seated at the end of a row of tables, and as one of the contestants walked by—a long, cool drink of water with an outrageous mop of crinkly blond hair—he looked down with a smile at Constance and said, in a polite drawl, "Good afternoon, Miss Keene."

I turned to Constance with a question in my eyes, for while there is certainly no rule against greeting judges personally, it is very rarely done. "That's the boy from Kilgore," she whispered. She was just as surprised as I.

The young man sat down at the keyboard, adjusting the stool to his elongated legs. "What would you like to play for us?" I asked.

"The Twelfth Liszt Rhapsody," he informed us evenly, and I could have sworn the long Texas jaw closed down like a clamp. Mine just about fell to the floor, and as I looked around I saw that the other judges were reacting identically. *He* knew, *we* knew, and we knew he knew that this was a daring choice. Ordinarily, a contestant tries to make a serious impression by first playing some serious classical work of Bach or Mozart or Beethoven. No one—well, almost no one—deliberately sets out to bowl over a jury with flashy gymnastics, for that is like impugning its musicianship or exposing one's own to doubt. I looked over at Mme. Isabelle Vengerova, the great teacher of piano who served as third judge. Her face, like ours, was full of misgivings over this strange young man who chose to start out with three strikes against him. Van never looked.

Fully expecting the Liszt to sound like a glass chandelier, I waved an arm and said, "If you wish." Van began. It took little more than a few seconds for us to realize what we were hearing and that actually we had been paid the highest of compliments. This young artist—for his artistry was evident the instant his huge hands touched the keys—had trusted us to recognize the musical purpose of his virtuosity, to understand his wish to endow this gaudy old war horse with nobility and expressive power. He came through handsomely. Only then did he turn to Bach, Mozart, Beethoven, Chopin, in a demonstration of pianism, sensitivity, and showmanship I have never known equaled in a competition. How well he succeeded was reflected later in Mme. Vengerova's bewildered question: "What for he wants the money to study? He is already an artist. All he needs now is more experience and repertoire."

We heard some remarkable piano playing from others, too, that day, but sorry as we were for several who fully deserved help, our duty was clear. Van stood out high above his nearest rival. He won the Chopin prize, both hands down.

Two years passed. I was invited to serve on the jury of the Leventritt Foundation, the oldest and most formidable international competition for young concert instrumentalists on this side of the Atlantic. The most coveted prize in the country, it offers the victor immediate engagements as soloist with the New York Philharmonic, the Cleveland, Pittsburgh, Buffalo, and Denver orchestras. Talent and proficiency are not sufficient to win the award. The contestant must, in the opinion of the judges, be fully equipped to fulfill the alpine demands of these important appearances and to sustain whatever concert career may arise from them.

So uncompromising are the standards by which the Leventritt Award is judged that for four previous years—from 1950 through 1953—no candidate had been able to meet them, although some thirty to forty talents from home and abroad had been auditioned each season. The jury of 1954 was just as exacting as any of its predecessors. It was composed of conductors George Szell, Dimitri Mitropoulos, and Leonard Bernstein; pianists Rudolf Serkin, Nadia Reisenberg, Leopold Mannes, and Eugene Istomin, himself the winner of the prize in 1943; violinist Alexander Schneider, violist Lillian Fuchs, and manager of the Philharmonic, Arthur Judson. My job was that of chairman.

The preliminary hearings occupied most of a week. And who showed up among the contestants but our young friend from Kilgore. His application listed the solo works and concertos he was prepared to play: Bach's E minor Partita, Mozart's Sonata, K. 330; Beethoven's "*Les Adieux*" Sonata; Ravel's Toccata and "*Jeux d'Eau*"; Hindemith's Third Sonata; Prokofiev's Sixth Sonata; Chopin's F minor Fantasy and B major Nocturne, Op. 62; and Liszt's Twelfth Rhapsody. Three concertos were listed: Mozart's D minor K. 466; Brahms' B-flat; Tchaikovsky's B-flat minor.

With typical dispatch Van impressed his excellence upon those members of the jury who had not heard him before. Early in the game Leopold Mannes was won over by the Beethoven. "This boy's the real thing," he enthused, "and he has one of the most eloquent left hands in the business." The Mozart sonata drew from Nadia Reisenberg the comment: "Exquisite. So much serenity and classic poise, yet it always sings." Everything Van did displayed his impressive command of the keyboard. At the same time, no matter what he played was graced by an unusual awareness of poetic values. His manner and manners charmed everyone. During one of the intermissions Mrs. Edgar Leventritt, who, with her daughter Rosalie Leventritt Berner, guides the foundation, said to me rapturously: "I just *love* the way he sits at the piano. Straight and white as a candle!"

Came the finals. As our long, cool drink of water threaded his way to the piano I scribbled a note to George Szell, who had just joined us: "Wait till you hear *this* boy. Remarkable." I must explain that we judges usually sat with several empty seats between us so we could listen more "alone" and with a sense of detachment. Notes were therefore often passed in lieu of whispered comments which might distract the contestants.

Van opened with the Tchaikovsky. After a time Szell slipped me the answer to my note: "He *is* remarkable," he had written. "No philosopher, in spite of the soulful facial expressions, but he makes beautiful sounds. Extraordinary skill and projection." In the last movement fire leaped from the instrument, and it was evident to us then—as it was later to become evident to spellbound audiences—that Van had a special flair for the Russian school. Leonard Bernstein said, "He really loves music, loves to play it, and loves the way *he* plays it. It's so honest and refreshing." Mitropoulos said, "He's fantastic. His playing is wizardry."

My own reactions were summed up in my notebook: "He arouses exceptional excitement. To his brilliant execution he has added unexpected qualities of taste and musicianship. *Born for the piano.*"

Before excusing Van from the platform we asked if he would care to play the last movement of the Brahms Concerto. I shall never forget his reply, for it was my first experience with the Van Cliburn tact and method of address, which have since become so famous.

"May I explain," he said quietly, "that I have been ill much of this past week. I feel it would be an injustice not only to myself but, far more important, to this great work and to the patience and integrity of this jury if I attempted to play the Brahms. Would you permit me to play something else?" It was all stated so gracefully yet firmly, with such implied confidence in our understanding and fairness—— What could we say?

I'll tell you what *I* said: I asked him to play the Liszt Twelfth Rhapsody. I smiled as I requested it, and Van grinned back. We both appreciated the irony of the situation. Two years before, I was aghast at the decision of a young man to start with a work that demands the finesse of a master if it is not to sound like an exhibitionistic chestnut. Now I was requesting it for my personal enjoyment. I'll never know which of us got more delight from the involuntary, audible cries of pleasure which came from the jurors during the stunning performance.

It was Mrs. Cliburn who enlightened me later that it was

she who advised Van to open contest performances with the Rhapsody. Judges usually allow contestants to choose their own first piece. After that they call their shots. Mrs. Cliburn feared that if Van didn't play the Liszt immediately he might never get the chance to play it; that the academicism might prevail which has led many musicians, who should know better, to scorn such works categorically as tinsel.

Van's approach to the piano was always in the grand old tradition. Now he has grown and matured. But way back in '54 the word *big* kept cropping up in our discussions, and the final collective verdict of that implacable group was that Van was a very big talent, with big style and the biggest potentialities. In addition, he played easily and naturally, as the birds sing. I recall, without remembering their sources, phrases like, "His poise is amazing. He has a heaven-sent radiance." Yes, Van had that black magic. Even then. Naturally, he ran away with the field.

Twenty years old and ready for the big break: Carnegie Hall, Mitropoulos conducting the Philharmonic, the program broadcast from coast to coast. On a Sunday afternoon that fall Van Cliburn stalked out on the stage, made a businesslike bow, and turned to the Steinway. The concerto chosen for this debut was the Tchaikovsky B-flat minor. At the end of the first movement cheers and bravos rang out from the orchestra as well as from the audience. At the conclusion of the work there were seven curtain calls. Seven.

The stalwart New York press was good, but guarded. Not raves, but qualified praise. The one metropolitan critic who went all out in torrential enthusiasm was Louis Biancolli, who reported to the readers of the *New York World-Telegram and Sun:* "This is one of the most genuine and refreshing keyboard talents to come out of the West—or anywhere else—in a long time. Van Cliburn is obviously going places, except that he plays as if he had already been there."

In the next four months Van played the other symphony engagements to which his prize entitled him. And what were the comments of the country's critics on this newcomer?

"There's a new wizard of the piano abroad in the land," said Elmore Bacon of the *Cleveland News* after he heard Van perform the Tchaikovsky under Szell.

Denver heard the Rachmaninoff Third Concerto, under conductor Saul Caston. Allen Young of the *Denver Post* alerted his readers with, "Tear out this name, write it somewhere, get to know it: Van Cliburn."

When Van appeared in Pittsburgh under William Steinberg's baton, Donald Steinfirst of the *Pittsburgh Post-Gazette* was forcibly struck by Van's similarity to a former musical magician: "Young Mr. Cliburn," he wrote, "a rangy 6-foot 4-inch Texan from the oil country, has the build of a basketball player, but I am sure more than one listener must have been inevitably drawn toward his resemblance to the legendary Franz Liszt as the latter burst upon a fashionable Parisian music world at the age of 20.

"We are told that the leonine handsome Liszt literally towered over his piano. No less does the blond, equally handsome young Mr. Cliburn. The word 'towered' is used musically. He literally enveloped the piano keyboard."

Irving Kolodin, music editor of *Saturday Review* sent a special dispatch to the *Dallas Morning News*:

> The likable young man . . . gave those who had never heard him a sense of renewed conviction that Texas does everything in a big way . . . A poetic percep-

tion uncommon in performers of years, a demonstration of truly outstanding talent . . . Strength, impact and personality . . .

This dispatch was requested by the paper's music critic, John Rosenfield, and in 1956 this "sage of the South" lived up to the appellation bestowed by an admiring musical world. Reviewing Van Cliburn a year and a half before Moscow, Rosenfield wrote:

His musical sensitivity, mature intelligence, poise, and mastery of his repertoire have been the means, and the brilliance and power have been only agencies.

Obviously the most widely held misapprehension of the Cliburn legend—that he was "discovered by the Russians"—is demolished by the record. Cliburn was discovered right in his own country, recognized by distinguished musicians, and hailed by American critics and audiences four years before he bought his ticket to Russia.

Why, then, did his 1958 triumph in the U.S.S.R. make front-page headlines? Why was his very existence such a howling surprise to our nation? Why were we caught with our cultural sights down?

A riddle perhaps, but no mystery.

While the Russians did not discover Van Cliburn they *did* embrace enthusiastically what we as a nation regard listlessly and relinquish casually—what their people value and our people ignore. The deplorable truth is that by the early spring of 1958 Van Cliburn's career was almost at a standstill. It had followed a pattern all too familiar to the very best American artistic talent. His great gift was on the point of becoming just another casualty of our publicity-enslaved cultural callousness. Then, in the nick of time, came the venturous trek to Moscow.

It will not lessen Cliburn's stature for us to realize that the day before his Moscow victory he was, in professional terms, exactly where most of the best American talent is today—struggling to gain or to hold what he had rightfully earned, hoping for the simple opportunity to do his work, to make a living at it, and to develop both in his art and in his career. Artistically, he was a supreme representative of the American standards that have produced many musicians who could make us proud anywhere, who deserve and could make full use of the finest opportunities.

Is it not reasonable that a climate which can produce such artists should also be able to appreciate them? And not only appreciate them but be anxious to recognize them as vital and precious resources that must not be squandered recklessly? Besides winning an artistic and political triumph Van Cliburn has ignited a new consciousness that arouses hope and optimism.

Shortly after the Moscow contest, and in answer to many of our good citizens who were asking sullen questions while nursing the bruises to their national pride, I said some of these things in an article for *The Reporter* magazine. It was entered intact into the *Congressional Record* by Senator Hubert Humphrey of Minnesota, as was other related material.

The fact that the Congress of the United States became concerned with the ups and downs of a piano player from Texas, and from his experiences hoped to deduce some lessons for the national welfare, indicates the temper of the times. Nothing could better demonstrate this young American's part in the dawning legislative recognition of art as a mainstream of life and of artists as vital national resources.

Undeniably, the phenomenal career of Van Cliburn has implications that extend far beyond the concert platform into our political, economic, and social status. What we can learn from it, how it may affect our cultural well-being, how its conclusions can be utilized to benefit other young artists whose combined raw talents represent a rich vein of our natural assets—these and their concomitants concern us all.

In this lies the moral of the Van Cliburn legend.

3

"The Eyes of Texas
Are upon You"

In 1939 the world's foremost pianist, Sergei Rachmaninoff, was engaged to play a recital in Shreveport, Louisiana. The great Russian exile had hastened back from Europe that summer. Loathing what he called the "Hitlerian weather," appalled at the clouds of war which billowed up behind him, Rachmaninoff buried his old resentment of the Bolsheviks and resolved to devote a sizable share of his American earnings to the Red Army.

Did Rildia Bee Cliburn of Shreveport and her fellow members on the music committee realize that the fee they paid the Master that evening might end up in Moscow? Would they have minded had they known? Probably not, for in those days many marriages were made against the Nazis and the Soviets were in-laws.

Of more concern to Mrs. Cliburn just then was that five-year-old Van had come down with some childhood ailment, and she had been forced to leave him at home in charge of a baby sitter. This was a keen disappointment to them both, for even at that age Van had been going with his mother to whatever concerts were available. Rachmaninoff, whose records were constantly played on the family phonograph, was already one of his musical gods.

Luckily the concert that night was being broadcast by the local radio station, so the patient was able to follow the program from his bed. Later when Mother came home, he was still wide awake and impatient for her to begin with her first-hand report. "I can still remember," an adult Van reminisced almost twenty years later, "that she told me how shy and kind Rachmaninoff was, and how sort of benign. After she had described how wonderful it was to talk to this truly great man, and had gone over the whole evening again and again, I thought for a time and said, 'Mommy, I think I want to be a concert pianist when I grow up. More than anything else in the world!'"

This childhood pronouncement made Mrs. Cliburn very happy, but it hardly came as much of a surprise. Two years before, she had been giving a piano lesson to one of her pupils and after finishing the session had gone to the kitchen. "Suddenly I heard, note by note, the little piece the pupil had played—the 'Arpeggio Waltz' by Crawford—being picked out on the piano. It was our Van, aged three. Right then I knew we had a budding pianist in the house."

Those who stress the influence of environment above innate talent can chalk one up for their side in the facts that Van was an only child, born after eleven years of marriage, and that teaching the piano was not only his mother's daily occupation but also the joy of her life. Moreover, day after day, all day long, neighborhood children came trooping in for lessons, deflecting Mrs. Cliburn's attention to themselves and earning her pride and approval when they brought good lessons. What more natural than that this alert child, watching every movement jealously, should try to become Mommy's best pupil himself? "I think I sort of prompted Mother to teach me when I was three years old," is how he remembers it. "I guess I thought if she could teach everybody else in the block—well then, she could certainly teach me."

So rivalry, as well as natural aptitude, may well have been an initial incentive. But to score a point for those who emphasize native gifts, the boy had absolute pitch and was phenomenally quick to learn. At the age of four he made his first public appearance, playing at a Shreveport college with Mother at a second piano. At five, when Mrs. Cliburn took him for registration at school, his first-grade teacher inquired if he could read. "Well no, ma'am," the chubby little boy answered gravely. "I can't read writing. But I can read music!" Mrs. Cliburn smiled modestly; the teacher stared.

Rildia Bee Cliburn, nee Rildia Bee O'Bryan, took piano as a child and had a passion for music. Later, deciding to teach for a living, she was sent up to New York to study under Arthur Friedheim, then a highly esteemed performer and teacher. Friedheim had studied in Europe directly under Liszt. Liszt had been a pupil of Czerny, father of scales. Czerny had been a pupil of Beethoven. And so a tradition came down in fairly unbroken lineage. Those who marvel that a young American should play so instinctively "in the grand manner" may see that from the start his training followed a distinguished bloodline, from Ludwig the Great down through Miss O'Bryan from Texas.

For a time Rildia Bee, in her devotion to the piano and its literature, half hoped that she herself might become a performing artist. But her parents were firm. "Young girls from good families just didn't do such things in those days —touring and all." She settled down to teach others to perform and eventually got married.

The O'Bryan family, Protestant-Irish in origin, was proud of its place in the development of Texas. Rildia Bee's grandfather, Dr. Solomon Green O'Bryan, had been a circuit rider and evangelist in the early days, a founder of the First Baptist Church in Waco, and Sam Houston's pastor. He also taught mathematics at Baylor University, in Independence, and was a founder of Waco University, which was merged with Baylor in 1886.

His son, Judge William Carey O'Bryan, was a graduate of Baylor and served in the Texas legislature, being a leader in the administrative revision of the Texas Penal Institutions. Judge O'Bryan became, in his later years, an elder statesman and adviser to Governor Patt Neff, Supreme Court Justice Tom Clark, and Representative Sam Rayburn. In his youth he had taught school for a while and married one of his pupils—Sirilda McClain. An actress of semiprofessional status in her early years and in later life a Texas historian, Sirilda was the daughter of Jack McClain, who owned twelve thousand acres of blackland where the towns of Moody and McGregor now stand. Today only eighty-eight acres of this once-vast tract remain in the family.

Van was six years old when his parents moved to Kilgore, Texas, a rig-studded oil town then with a census of 6,960, where Mr. Cliburn became a "landman" for the Magnolia Petroleum Company, an affiliate of Socony Mobil.

All over America there are fathers like Mr. Cliburn—devoted family men, sensible, hard-working businessmen who still quietly cherish some dream of ambition they had to forego. Cliburn senior had hoped in his youth to be a missionary doctor. Economics decreed otherwise. He laid down his aspirations and transferred the ideal to his son.

When Van embraced music instead as a career the father showed resistance for a while. Hopefully he brought home a pair of roller skates, a shiny new bike. A year or two later he had to give them away, hardly even broken in. On one occasion when he came home from work to find the boy sagged over the keyboard, dog-tired after a full day's practice, he remonstrated gently—why not choose something less demanding in a career? The limp figure shot erect, and Van cried indignantly: "Daddy, don't say such things! I'm going to become a concert pianist!"

It should be marked to Mr. Cliburn's everlasting credit that, despite his shrewd distrust of the concert stage as a means to a living, he gave in gracefully, once he realized his son was wholeheartedly dedicated. Not only gave in but pitched in, up to the elbows. First, he dived into an insurance program he could hardly afford, to protect the boy's future. Then onto the garage he built a studio in which Van could practice. There were two pianos in that studio, and two inside the house—four in all, which argues that the family, though never well-to-do, was not on short rations. But even so, there is no stronger desire among such American families than to give their children every educational advantage.

The spirit of that home was one of love and loyalty, of faith and enthusiasm. It left its mark on Van. What he is and what he does are easily explainable if we look into the Cliburn household, into the salient influences and wholesome origins which went to form the make-up and character of a very unusual young man.

The constant preoccupation of the home was music, providing a perfect hothouse atmosphere for development and study. Mrs. Cliburn had obviously worked out a splendid method of teaching, to judge by her son's exceptionally solid technical foundations today and his firm view of technique as merely a means to musical ends. Other pupils were continuously at hand to contribute the necessary competitive spur, and Teacher herself was always somewhere close enough to hear incipient errors and supply the corrections. For inspiration a bust of Chopin gazed down from the piano top.

From the beginning the boy never was nagged into practicing. As a toddler he would tug at his mother's skirt and say, "Mommy, I want my piano lesson." Later, when he grew old enough to join in games with neighborhood children, Mrs. Cliburn never called him to come in the house and practice. "I would simply sit down and start playing," she says. "He would always come running."

"I loved being taught by my mother," Van explains, "because she never treated me as a child, never flattered me or patronized me. When I had a lesson, seated on the piano bench with my ankles interlocked to keep my legs from dangling, she'd say, 'That's pretty fair.' Or, 'That's coming along nicely.' No fussing. No feathers. The people I hated were the ones who patted me on the head and made me feel like a dog act. You know?"

From earliest memory Van was given an almost adult sense of his own importance in the family and of the worthwhileness of everything he did. When he sat down at the piano, even to practice scales, the two grownups would stop whatever they were doing and constitute his audience. Before he could walk they carried him to church to sit with them in their pew; and as soon as he was old enough to sing he joined them in the choir. It is impossible that the boy was ever, during his formative years, shushed or pushed aside or told to go away and not bother his elders. He always was "wanted." And this, in the present-day Van, is reflected in the sunny aplomb with which he enters a room or a concert hall, whether in Moscow or Washington or Baraboo, Wisconsin—invariably poised and eager and certain of his welcome. The grown-up Van Cliburn sincerely loves people; so it follows, naturally, that people love him. Not just singly, but in droves.

Perhaps the most remarkable phase of his education as a child was his training in manners. From his outgoing mother he learned to turn a compliment so deftly that the happy recipient could go on basking for days in its rosy afterglow. And he learned both the charm and value of unexpected gifts—flowers and candy for presents, whatever the state of the budget. By Christmas morning the drugstore near their house would be stripped of its supply of Whitman's Sampler chocolates, all bought up by the Cliburns and delivered around town in person.

To this day red roses are the "Van Cliburn trademark." Even after the return from Moscow, and at the end of a harrowing day which had included, for him, a recording session and a television appearance with Ed Murrow, he appeared after midnight at the door of our apartment, weaving with weariness but holding a bowl of red roses in his hands. He knew that Constance, who had undergone surgery, would be home from the hospital next morning, and he wanted to make sure the flowers would be there to greet

39

her. All arranged, too. Such thoughtfulness, though by now a part of his nature, is a vestige of the Southern chivalry instilled in his boyhood.

While still in knee pants Van was accustomed to meeting quite celebrated musicians and discussing his work with them. It was nothing unusual for the family to drive all the way to Dallas, for example, a round trip of six hours, so that mother and son could attend a concert. Afterward they would go backstage to "talk shop" with the performer, as they did with Constance.

Colonel D. Harold Byrd of Dallas, a great admirer of José Iturbi, recalls the time he engaged that artist to play in his city in 1946. The colonel had reserved a suite for Iturbi at the Hotel Adolphus and was up there waiting for the pianist to dress for dinner, when there came a knock at the door. The colonel strode to open it and was confronted by a curly-headed lad of approximately twelve.

"My name's Van Cliburn," the boy said politely. "I came to play for Mr. Iturbi and ask him a question."

"Well, come in, come in," the colonel answered affably. "Mr. Iturbi's inside shaving, but there's the piano. Can you play my favorite piece, '*Clair de Lune*'?"

The boy began to play "*Clair de Lune,*" and before he had finished Iturbi emerged from the bathroom, wiping the last of the lather from his face. "Fine, fine!" he said approvingly after the final chord had been resolved. "Done with real feeling! You're a talented youngster—keep on working. Who is your teacher?"

"My mother," said Van.

"I'd love to meet her," Iturbi responded. "I have some things to attend to right now, but could you get your mother and return here in forty-five minutes?"

At the indicated time Van and his mother were at the hotel. Although Iturbi complimented Mrs. Cliburn heartily on the way she had taught Van she asked a question that had been troubling her for some time: should she not now, at this stage, give Van over to some other teacher?

"My dear," said Iturbi, "I have heard so many people! You simply don't know what a fine teacher you are. It would be an injustice to send your son to anyone else." Then he added: "If you ever get to the West Coast, please come to see me. I'd like Van to play for me again and for all of you to meet my sister Amparo."

Three months later the family went to Denver, where Mr. Cliburn had to attend a company convention. "While there," says Van, "we decided to go on to the West Coast for a vacation and with the hope of seeing Iturbi again. We did see him, but he was working on a film. I came down with a terrible cold, a polio epidemic was reported, and so I didn't get to play for him." After two days they went back to Texas.

Mrs. Cliburn frequently wondered if her son should not be exposed to some other tutelage. Van always refused. "I used to threaten to give up the piano entirely when she tried to give me away to another teacher," he says.

However, when he was thirteen he accompanied his mother up to New York for summer sessions at Juilliard. Mrs. Cliburn says frankly that, though she enjoyed and profited from the master classes she attended, her real object was to "case" the school faculty and try to decide on an instructor she felt would be right for her son.

Van, in the meantime, took academic subjects: harmony, theory, sight reading, dictation, keyboard harmony, and ensemble. School officials, consulting his old records, say he "did brilliantly." The next summer he came up to study with the eminent Ernest Hutcheson, Juilliard's scholarly taskmaster, who, in spite of his own superb artistry, was always more interested in the intellectual and technical achievements of talent than in talent itself. There is reason to assume that Van did not exactly quiver with excitement under Hutcheson's objective guidance—by no means the only gifted student to react the same way—and after five lessons Van declared himself out. Mother, however, was learning many vital things and not only finished the course with "Hutchie" but also won herself a dividend—Van's final lesson.

It was this summer that Olga Samaroff, another of Juilliard's distinguished instructors, heard enthusiastic reports about Van. Mme. Samaroff, who came from San Antonio, Texas—and whose name had once been Lucy Hickenlooper and later Mme. Leopold Stokowski—offered the boy a scholarship without even hearing him. She died, however, before he could avail himself of the opportunity. After that he refused even to consider another teacher and returned to Texas to enter high school.

Nobody has ever been stupid enough to underestimate Van Cliburn's intelligence. He has been aptly described as having "a mind like a whippet." His mother maintains that at the piano all she ever had to do was to show him something once, and never again. Associates declare he is blessed with total recall. By the help of a summer course he shot through Kilgore High in only three years yet maintained such high grades that he was one of the elite segment of pupils nominated by the faculty to the National Honor Society, a distinction based on marks of A's and B's, plus outstanding qualities of character and leadership. Briefly, he topped off high school with a summer session at Kilgore Junior College, where he studied freshman English and psychology—one of only two students who merited A in these subjects.

Van always says, "I can't learn anything that doesn't interest me. My imagination has to be stirred." Latin, possibly because of its highly inflected structure, appealed to his sense of rhythm and form. "I was pretty good at that," he once told me—and to prove it jumped up and rattled off, in Latin, the salute to the flag!

Being Van, of course, he was very gregarious and popular at school. It was not easy for a boy so extrovert by nature and so fond of mixing to be kept away from sports. Yet he had to avoid activities which might endanger his hands. A happy solution was found by permitting him to tootle a clarinet in football parades. Soon he had talked the band into the more ambitious project of accompanying him in a concerto at a college in Denton, Texas. When the concert was over a student interviewed Van for the college paper. Was it true, she wanted to know, that he had played for Iturbi? And what did Iturbi say?

"Aah," said Van, wriggling uncomfortably. "He said I was okay. . . ."

More than one coach has studied Van's skyscraper anatomy and swift co-ordination, only to deplore the loss to sports of a potentially great athlete. A Notre Dame coach was sitting in the audience one night when Van gave a concert in South Bend, Indiana. "The piano sure robbed somebody of a wonderful basketball player," he mourned as the tremendous hands went skimmering over the black and white keys.

High school coach Bradford at Kilgore used to watch Van

when he dropped into the gym occasionally to fool around with the boys and pop a ball or two into the basket. The ease and accuracy with which he achieved this were maddening; yet, according to Bradford, most everybody understood why Van firmly resisted going out for the team. "Ordinarily," he says, "you take somebody that's a genius, there's something peculiar about him. You know, something different. But not Van. He was a good, solid boy."

The only extracurricular activities to which the good, solid boy seems to have given much time were the high school paper and theatricals. As a staff member of the *Kilgore Mirror* he wrote editorials and had one of his poems, "The Void," published in the high school anthology. He was president of the Thespian Society, and although his troupe never got beyond the rehearsal stage he experimented with comedy in the Clifton Webb role in *Sitting Pretty* and with heavy drama in the Ralph Bellamy role in *Tomorrow the World*. He has never fully abandoned a furtive belief that he would have made a good actor, and with his high powers of personal projection he possibly might.

In his early teens the lad who had looked so cherubic at the keyboard began to shoot upward as though he had been fed gibberellin. His astonished metabolism was permitted no time to place flesh on the accelerating bones, and so at sixteen Van was a long and lanky fellow, all elbows and knees, with feet that required size-twelve shoes. He also had more than a normal quota of carbuncles and boils, a nuisance he has not yet entirely worked out of his system. Therefore when Van characterizes these years as a "rough time" he is referring to the pangs of adolescence, worse than usual in his case because, as he says, "You can't love music enough to want to play it without some kids thinking you're queer or something." His hair then, as now—unless constantly sheared down by a ruthless barber—was a tawny mane that bushed out like a lion's.

Nevertheless, according to the girls who met him at parties, Van was a gay companion and an exceptionally fine dancer. He played the popular hits of the day, loved a good time, and is remembered as "one of the most congenial boys at school." But work came first. He got up early enough to put in an hour or two of practice before school each morning and got in several more hours later on in the day. Sometimes after practice he would "relax" at the piano by breaking into Gershwin or Berlin, singing as he went. Since Mother's teaching schedule left little time for cooking, the family often had dinner at Mrs. Lake's tiny café, where Van especially enjoyed the pot roast with its side-dressing of turnip greens and corn bread.

Van played all over his state throughout the years of his childhood, and Texans had begun to "brag on him" by the time he was twelve. Later, in 1947, he notified his mother he was ready to compete for the Texas State Prize, which offered an appearance with the Houston Symphony under Ernest Hoffman. Mrs. Cliburn tried to discourage him at first, thinking him too young for the grueling work involved in preparing for such a contest. When he insisted she marked on a blackboard the number of days remaining before the competition and crossed off each day of practice as it passed. At the end of twenty-one days Van had memorized the Tchaikovsky B-flat minor Concerto. With it he not only won the finals in the statewide contest but received a standing ovation from the orchestra when he played it in Houston. Later the same season he performed in Carnegie Hall as the

Texas winner of the National Music Festival's nationwide sweepstakes to discover juvenile talent.

In April of 1952 he won the G. B. Dealey Memorial Award, established by the late publisher of the *Dallas Morning News*. This award brings a cash prize of five hundred dollars, which was increased, in Van's case, by a spontaneous gift from Colonel Byrd. It also gave him the opportunity of being heard with the Dallas Symphony, under Walter Hendl's baton. He played the MacDowell Second in D minor. This was two months before we heard him in New York at the Chopin competition.

The boy was busily piling up credits.

4

Tests and Contests

After Labor Day in 1951 music students from the far-flung counties of the United States and music teachers fresh from summer vacations converged on the Juilliard School of Music in upper Manhattan. Among the teachers was Mme. Rosina Lhevinne, widow and duo-piano partner of famed Josef Lhevinne and instructor of only the most advanced students. Among the incoming pupils was one Van Cliburn who, with his mother, was temporarily ensconced at the Buckingham Hotel.

Mrs. Cliburn remembers:

When the registration card from Juilliard arrived at the hotel, they discovered that Van was assigned, not to Mme. Lhevinne as they had assumed and requested, but to one of her assistants. Alarm and dismay! After three years of traveling all the way from Texas, for practically the sole purpose of choosing a teacher, they felt themselves betrayed. "You just get on that phone and talk to Mme. Lhevinne yourself," Mrs. Cliburn advised. "I'm sure she'll understand."

Van put the call through, but Mme. Lhevinne explained that her classes were unfortunately filled. She had not been present when the first student auditions had been held at Juilliard, so she had not heard him play. "But," she suggested, "perhaps I can take you next year."

Van remembers saying:

"But I *must* study with you, Mrs. Lhevinne. Even if you can give me only ten minutes a week I'll consider myself your pupil. However," he told her, "if you definitely can't take me and I go to another teacher, I'll stay with that teacher until I graduate. What I want you to know about me, Mrs. Lhevinne, is that I'm very loyal."

Mme. Lhevinne remembers:

She was standing by the school elevator one day when a tall, shockheaded young man with a long, buoyant stride bore down upon her. "Honey," he said with a smile, "I'm here to study with you."

In any event, what threw the balance in Van's favor, in the face of filled schedules, was that two other Lhevinne students from Texas, Jeaneane Dowis and James Mathis, both outstandingly gifted pianists and Dealey Award winners, spoke up in Van's behalf. He was a tremendous talent, they assured Mme. Lhevinne glowingly. At least, would she hear him? She agreed to that, and he played—what else?— the Liszt Twelfth Rhapsody. Once again Old Faithful worked its infallible charm. Somehow Madame found a place on her schedule for Van Cliburn.

I have since asked Mme. Lhevinne: "What first impressed you about Van?"

"His big, sweeping approach," she answered without hesitation. "And also I could see he had great sensitivity."

Mrs. Cliburn found lodgings for Van in the apartment of

Allen and Hazel Spicer on Claremont Avenue, not far from
the school. There Van was provided with his own bath and
big comfortable room, with ceiling so high that even his
giraffe-like height could pass beneath the lintel of the door
without ducking. But the thing that had most pleased Mrs.
Cliburn's eye on the initial tour of inspection was the venerable Chickering grand that stood in the living room. Would
Van be permitted an hour or two a day of practice on that?

"Yes," Mrs. Spicer agreed, but on one condition—that he
didn't play scales.

Next to the carillon and the pipe organ, I suppose, the
piano presents the greatest instrumental problem to those
who have to practice. You can't carry the beast around; you
have to use it when and where you find it. Van, suddenly
deprived of his garage-studio at home, was forced to a catch-
as-catch-can pursuit of time and place for study: practice
rooms at Juilliard when not occupied by others; by-the-hour
studios in mid-town Manhattan; and, with blankets over
and under the Chickering to deaden the sound, occasional
evening sessions at home which had to stop promptly at
ten o'clock, in consideration of the neighbors.

The stately Chickering with its mellow tone blanched under Van's exuberant attacks until it threatened to collapse.
This disaster was avoided when Van became a "Steinway
artist," after his Leventritt victory had motivated the Stein-
ways to send him up one of their pianos. The valiant old
family instrument, of course, could not be evicted, so the
movers lined up both pianos, cheek by jowl, until they took
up not more than half of the living room. "The place looks
awful!" Hazel Spicer wailed. "Like a furniture warehouse!"

But Van was ecstatic. "It's beautiful, honey," he assured
her. "It looks just like home!"

Almost the first thing Van did after establishing himself as a resident New Yorker was to get his church membership transferred from Kilgore to Manhattan. Calvary Baptist Church on West 57th Street is practically next door to Steinway Hall and within a formal nod of Carnegie Hall, its dowdy but dignified neighbor up the street. Here Van felt at home and was wholeheartedly welcomed from the very beginning.

Accustomed from infancy to a regular and intensive church attendance with his parents, Van did not consider it burdensome in New York to subway down to church every Wednesday evening for service, Thursday evening for choir practice, and twice on Sunday. Nor did he consider it strange to give the church one tenth of whatever fees he earned by playing or whatever prize moneys he won in competitions, since his parents had been tithers long before his birth. Later he often doubled the amount.

"We've been tithing all our lives," says Father Cliburn proudly. "But Van, he's a double tither. Not ten per cent of his earnings, but twenty." What he forgot to add was that Van pays this percentage on gross, not net . . . right off the top.

During the early days at Calvary, Van formed strong friendships, and these ties seem destined to endure untarnished, no matter what. His friends there say, "We do not see so much of Van now, since Moscow—he is so busy. But we are here, and he knows it, and he knows we'll still be here whenever he comes."

Soon after Van's arrival he met a girl from back home who was studying voice at Juilliard—Donna Sanders from Greenville, Texas. Willowy, brunette, attractive, and talented, she was also a soloist at Calvary Church. The two had much in common and, though never formally engaged, arrived, in time, at an unofficial "understanding." Van was serious enough about it to think favorably of marriage and to probe the possibilities of bringing a bride to the Claremont Avenue apartment.

The age-old struggle of marriage vs. career arose. But this one was modern style, for the girl, who could dance as well as sing, found a place in the cast of *The Saint of Bleecker Street*. When it became marriage vs. two careers the latter won out. While the situation hung in balance Van's parents seem to have handled it well. They merely suggested that the youngsters wait for one year. They agreed. Donna eventually married an actor, and Van has since been heard to remark, "I don't think I'll ever get married." We'll see.

In celebration of Van's capture of the Chopin award he was taken by Polish friends down to the Asti in Greenwich Village, a restaurant well known to singers and musicians. At once he endeared himself to owner Adolphi Mariani, both by his way with the big piano in the middle of the floor and with the big steak in the middle of his plate. Though Van can dine cheerfully on a couple of hamburgers —and still does at rehearsals or when time presses—he is a rewarding man to feed, as an increasing number of maîtres d'hôtel can testify. He loves good food and can handle it in quantities. Soon he was among the considerable number of young artists who go to the Asti, eat there when they are hungry, play there when they feel like it, and pay—after they have won gold medals at Moscow. But *never*, as reported in one national magazine, do they do anything so crass as "play for their suppers."

There is finesse in such matters. For example, when Van was going around with Donna he would sometimes call up manager Gil Gallagher in the late afternoon, tell him he would like to bring his girl down to dinner but didn't have much money—and could you kindly go light on the bill? Of course!—and no embarrassing bill was brought to the table. At other times he would show up with conductor Walter Hendl, whom he had known since his appearance with the Dallas Symphony, or with Jerome Hines, basso of the Metropolitan Opera, or with a table full of friends; and, the mood being right, he would play on and on till time for lights out. But he never used liquor. His own high spirits were intoxication enough. Van is an incorrigible mineral-water man, a Seven-Upper—a teetotaler both by preference and religious conviction.

During his second and third years at Juilliard he spent his summers at Chautauqua, playing with the Chautauqua Symphony Orchestra, which Hendl conducted. Mrs. Stephen I. Munger of Dallas had a summer home at the lake, and Van lived there as a house guest.

Texas was well represented at the resort while Van was there, as noted in a music review written by David Holden for the *Chautauquan:*

> Sunday decorum was thrown to the winds at the conclusion of the Chautauqua Symphony Orchestra's concert as a packed Amphitheater called Van Cliburn back to the stage six times with a prolonged ovation. Texans in the crowd seemed barely able to keep from drawing their "shootin' irons," and "whoopies" trembled on their lips. For the 18-year-old citizen of the Lone Star State had completed a terrific performance of a terrific concerto.

Terrific concerto? The Tchaikovsky.

Gil Gallagher of the Asti, a part-time baritone, also spent his summers at Chautauqua, coaching opera. Back in town Gallagher was preparing to sing the role of the Sheriff of Nottingham in *Robin Hood*. He telephoned Van one night and asked if he would come down to the Asti and go over the music with him. Van not only came down and went over the music but stayed up most of the night playing the entire De Koven score on the piano and singing the sólos. Before he left, the whole thing was on tape. What an interesting item that would make today, Gallagher thought. But when he went to find it one A.M. (after Moscow) he found to his horror that he had erased it in using the tape over again. Lost to the world, one Cliburn curio—a very odd find, it might have been, for the collectors.

Although Van, upon his entrance to Julliard, had undertaken the academic course leading to a bachelor of science degree he changed over in his second year to the conservatory course. This curriculum, granting a diploma but imposing a lighter load in semester hours, left him more free time for outside work and playing engagements.

Scholarships at the Juilliard are given only on the basis of musical ability, the amount of money varying with each student's needs. Upon entrance Van was accorded a scholarship-in-name, but as Mrs. Cliburn explains with a twinkle, "We weren't quite poor enough to qualify for a grant." He was still a freshman at Juilliard when he won the Dealey Award of $500, upped by Colonel Byrd, and the Chopin Scholarship of $1000. This is not chicken feed for a teen-ager. He was a sophomore when he won a grant from the Olga Samaroff Foundation and captured first place in Juilliard's concerto contest. The concerto, which was broadcast over the municipal station, WNYC, was——? Right. The Tchaikovsky.

Two unexpected strokes of luck came to Van, also in that second year: Van Cliburn Day—the first on record—was proclaimed in Kilgore on April 9, 1953, when Van returned after a two-year absence to play before his fellow townsmen, and a purse of six hundred dollars was presented to him from the community.

The occasion got off to a shaky start. Thirty minutes past concert time the hero of the evening had not yet arrived at the college auditorium. Meanwhile, fifteen hundred nettled East Texans were twisting in their seats, concert chairman Frances Gertz and her committee were "sweating blood." Tempers were not helped too much when rumor circulated that the artist, blissfully free of nerves and a sense of time, was still at home on the phone, talking long-distance to his girl in New York! When Van finally showed up some of his audience was tired of sitting—a condition which he quickly remedied by striding to the piano and thundering out the rousing chords of "The Star-Spangled Banner." To the last true patriot, they leaped to their feet. . . .

All was forgiven, however, as the recital proceeded—a beautiful and beautifully played program comprising Bach's C minor Toccata, Mozart's C major Sonata, K. 330, Prokofiev's Sixth Sonata, two études and the F minor Fantasy by Chopin, Ravel's *"Une barque sur l'ocean"* and Toccata. When the last riotous roars of applause had subsided, Elmer Scott of Dallas, for whom Scott Hall in that city is named, spoke of the powerful impression Van had made when he played with the Dallas Symphony, and said to the pianist: "Tonight you came nearer than any other artist to making me like Ravel."

Van's parents, called onstage during the intermission, stood beside Van while he was presented with the check as a "gift from the people of your home town . . . in appreciation of your work and the acclaim you have brought to Kilgore." The money was contributed, explained Mrs. Raymond Whittlesey, president of the Kilgore Music Club, to help further Van's musical career. This tribute of their neighbors, so sincere and spontaneous, was possibly the most emotionally stirring moment in the lives of Mr. and Mrs. Cliburn. Van, equally moved, thanked all who had "made this wonderful day possible" and dedicated his final encores to the Kilgore Music Club: Chopin's A-flat Polonaise and—Liszt's Twelfth Rhapsody.

The first time Van was scheduled to take part in a concert at Juilliard he was twenty minutes late in making an appearance. He had decided to nap for a few minutes and had gone right on sleeping. The "late Mr. Cliburn," as he has become known to a widening circle of associates, has no sense of time, no subliminal clock ticking away in the back of his head to warn him of the hours. Partly to blame for this is his power of concentration—nothing else exists but the matter at hand. Part is simply his mercurial nature. "I procrastinate and am late," he admitted honestly to the room full of press men he had kept waiting. "I live for the moment." The result is that he drives hostesses to mayhem and is always in boiling water with friends. Since Moscow a growing sense of public responsibility has nagged him into herculean efforts to cure this self-confessed fault; but it is a slow, stubborn battle.

In his second year Van was recommended by Juilliard as an entrant in the Michaels Award competition in Chicago, which grants $1000 for first prize plus a summer performance at Ravinia Park with the Chicago Symphony. Additional engagements are guaranteed with Pittsburgh, Minneapolis, and other major city orchestras. Preliminary hearings are held in New York and Chicago, in which some two to three hundred young instrumentalists take part. Out of these about twenty-five survive into the semifinals, which are held in closed session in Chicago. The finals are public concerts; and in this respect the Michaels, alone of all our American competitions, resembles the big public contests of Brussels, Warsaw and Moscow.

Knowing how large a part religious faith plays in Van's every action, Mme. Lhevinne said to her pupil one day while he was preparing for the fray: "I suppose you're praying you'll win in Chicago?"

"No," he answered quietly. "I'm praying God to give me the strength to bear it if I don't come through."

This has always been his prayer before every test of fire. But this once he needed it. For the first time in his life he failed to breeze away with first prize.

The decision, especially in the light of later events, has never sat well with Roger Dettmer, music critic of the *Chicago American*. Nor has what Dettmer termed the "amateur management" of the coveted award. Reporting the pianistic victory of Augustin Anievas over Olegna Fuschi at the 1958 finals, Dettmer wrote: ". . . a chorus of spontaneous hoots punctuated the applause" when the winner was announced. After Moscow acclaimed Van Cliburn with the verdict, "We chose the most deserving of the deserving," Dettmer decided to look back into the records and disinter the particulars of the 1953 conclave. His conclusion was given wide circulation in the August 10, 1958, issue of *The New York Times*:

Mr. Cliburn's case is especially interesting and, I think, illustrative of the Michaels method. Only 19 at finals time, he came recommended by Mme. Lhevinne and Mark Schubart.

Judges at the spring semi-finals had written on their tot-sheets, among various germane or gratuitous comments, "musicianship fine . . . technique excellent . . . fine natural talent" (Izler Solomon), "technique adequate . . . mannered playing" (George Kuyper, Chicago Symphony manager), "technique very sure and solid, excellent projection . . . very promising . . . highly gifted pianist" (the late Felix Borowski, composer and then dean of Chicago critics).

Later that year the finalists, including Mr. Cliburn, faced eight judges. Mr. Cliburn played music, during the decisive closed session, by Chopin, Liszt, Beethoven ("Les Adieux" Sonata) and Prokofiev (Sonata No. 6). It was unanimously decided, however, before the evening concert that Mr. Olefsky would be winner because of his greater age, maturity and professional attainments.

That evening fellow-judges were jolted from their unanimity when Dr. Borowski shifted his vote from Mr. Olefsky to Mr. Cliburn, explaining later to his wife, "I could not vote against that great talent."

Paul Olefsky is not a pianist but a 'cellist—a splendid one, too—who was then in the armed services and who since has become first 'cellist of the Detroit Symphony Orchestra. No one disputes this fine artist's right to significant recognition. Surely, least of all Van. Although he sometimes remarks that he has "never lost a contest to another pianist," he has never questioned the Michaels decision. Mrs. Cliburn, who went to Chicago for the finals, told the judges afterward that she was "just as happy Van was not a winner all the time—one has to learn to lose, too."

Nevertheless, the verdict initiated considerable reverberation, which provides evidence that on the sole occasion when Van's competitive supremacy was not acknowledged potent protests arose from authoritative sources.

By now word was percolating quietly around the rather insular music world of New York that an extraordinary pair of hands—spanning an octave and a fifth—was at work around Juilliard. Rumors had already reached the ears of concert manager William M. Judd when Mark Schubart, dean of Juilliard, phoned him to say: "I've never done this before, but there's a pianist here named Van Cliburn I think you ought to hear."

"I've been hearing *about* him," Judd said. "Do you think I could get a listen in some informal way?"

Schubart said that would be easy. Mme. Lhevinne frequently gave her pupils lessons in the auditorium instead of in her small studio. If Judd would like to come up and join him for one of those sessions, they would be inconspicuous in the big hall.

Van walked out on the school stage one afternoon to play a Mozart and a Prokofiev sonata for Madame, totally unaware that one of the country's most astute and influential concert managers was listening from a back seat, out of sight in the shadows. Bill Judd was sold. As he explained later: "This was the only artist I was completely certain about the first time I heard him."

Judd did not anticipate—how could he, a partner of one of the music industry's top-ranking firms?—that his next job would be to try to sell *Van*. At that time Judson, O'Neill and Judd was a division of Columbia Concerts, Inc., which managed such stars as Lily Pons, Richard Tucker, Mischa Elman, Jascha Heifetz, Rudolf Serkin. Almost any eighteen-year-old student with but one large foot planted on the bottommost rung of the long upward ladder would have happily signed with his life's blood if proffered a contract. Van thanked them kindly and said he'd like to think about the matter. "Thinking about a matter," in the Cliburn vocabulary, means seeking advice of all and sundry while action is deferred.

For more than a year Judson, O'Neill and Judd pursued their golden quarry with dinner invitations, concert tickets, revised clauses and options and other inducements until his shaggy head should have been turned. But Van did not sign. Nor did he refuse. He merely ate their dinners gratefully and kept on practicing.

"How good, really, do you think Van is?" Allen Spicer asked Bill Judd one evening when he had dropped in at the Claremont Avenue apartment. "Tell it to me so that a businessman can understand it."

"Well, let me put it this way," Judd replied. "First, he is one whale of a piano player. And second, he's better than even *he* knows."

Van graduated from Juilliard on May 28, 1954, receiving the Carl M. Roeder Memorial Award, given for "outstanding achievement in piano" and the Frank Damrosch Scholarship, which entitled him to one year of post-graduate study. About this time he let it be known that he was going out after the Leventritt Award in the fall; and with this announcement the patience of his would-be managers nearly blew up.

In our country the onus of amateurism has always hung darkly upon competitions and their participants, principally insofar as American management is concerned. And although Van was still technically a student it is indicative of how highly Judson, O'Neill and Judd appraised his potential, that already they esteemed him as a professional who would be well advised to avoid competitions. They were also fearful that he might become typed as a chronic contestant. Especially in view of *l'affaire Michaels*.

But "Van has always made his own decisions," as Bill Judd points out with cheerless resignation. All arguments were vain; Van filled out the Leventritt blank and sent it in.

His application was one of forty-eight received by the Foundation that year. Rosalie Leventritt Berner, the acting director, remembers that she was packing up her brief case one day, preparing to attend a meeting, when she noticed that one contestant's folder was fatter and heavier than almost all the others put together. Curious, she opened it. Dozens of newspaper clippings tumbled out, seemingly culled from every corner of Texas and detailing the triumphs of one Van Cliburn whose seraphic face, at various stages of development, gazed up at her from pictures. A tremendous coverage, but—save for Chopin and Dealey—smalltime stuff. Smiling to herself, Mrs. Berner tucked the dossier back into her brief case and lugged it to the meeting.

During the trials of the Leventritt auditions Van would telephone his closest friends from Calvary and remind them eagerly: "You won't forget to pray for me, will you? It buoys me up when I know you're praying." Brought up to believe that all his talent was a direct gift from God, he had always been reminded by his mother, even in the heat of applause, "Never forget Whence all this comes." He never does.

"Music is God's language," he is fond of quoting; and the great power of his communication with people in terms of that language is undoubtedly due, to an incalculable degree, to the confidence and radiance born of this belief.

On the day of the Leventritt finals, after Van had finished playing for the jurors, he returned to the Claremont Avenue apartment to await the decision. All afternoon he stewed around, unable to do anything but listen for the phone to ring. Finally, Bill Judd called, and over the extension in his room Van heard him say, "Congrats! Arthur Judson just got back to the office and said the verdict was unanimous."

"Hazel, Hazel, I've won, I've won!" he cried out to Mrs. Spicer, erupting into the living room and flinging his arms around her. "Isn't it wonderful? . . . Go get dressed up and we'll go out to dinner!"

"Oh no, Van, go call up a girl," Mrs. Spicer protested. He should really celebrate, she was thinking, and it'll be so much more fun with youngsters his own age.

But Van insisted. "You go get ready—I've got to call up Rosina right away."

He began to dial Mme. Lhevinne's number, then changed his mind. "No. It's no good," he decided, dropping the phone. "I'm going up there and tell her myself." Grabbing his coat from the closet, he ran out, calling, "Wait for me. I'll be back!"

When Mme. Lhevinne answered the throbbing, frenzied ringing of her doorbell she was nearly bowled over by the onrushing figure in the big, burly overcoat. "Honey, I got it! Honey, I won!" The long arms wrapped about her and whirled her around the floor. Together—when at last they were able to control their hilarity—they called Kilgore to share the news with Van's parents.

Finally, Van sank down on the sofa and hid his head in his hands. "Oh, *what* a responsibility," he said. "What a *dreadful* responsibility!" He lapsed into an awed silence, his eyes peering into the unforeseeable future. Suddenly he rose and said he'd better be going along.

But before returning home he paid one more visit. His good friend Clifford Tucker, organist at Calvary, was ill at the time, and Van knew how much the Leventritt news would cheer him. Before starting out with the Spicers to celebrate the prize that launched his professional career he stopped in at the hospital.

It was typical. The man himself was running true to form. The career—on schedule.

5

Coming of Age

Although I have screamed at friends who swallowed Shostakovich's startling statement that Van Cliburn "earned his first wide and entirely deserved recognition among us here in Moscow," it contained just enough truth to hurt. The achievements of our native artists have always been among our better kept secrets.

The annual press release announcing the Fifteenth Leventritt International Competition of 1954, like all those in its fifteen-year history, was pruned down to a few sentences, tucked away in the musical miscellany columns of one or two of the best New York papers. And Van Cliburn's newsworthy capture of America's top music-performance award that year received the absent treatment or the casual treatment accorded all those before and after who won similar distinction—until the nineteenth annual contest came along, in September of 1958. By then all of us had had quite a jolt. But the '57 winner, pianist Anton Kuerti, was disposed of in one paragraph by the foremost New York daily, without even mention of a jury whose names would have informed its readers of the stringency of the test and the magnitude of the accomplishment. That's one reason why his name may be unfamiliar, like that of Van Cliburn three years before. When Van won, the jury was mentioned but the award was said to entitle him "to appear as soloist with the Philharmonic Symphony during the 1954–55 season." That the Leventritt Award also carried appearances with the orchestras of Cleveland, Pittsburgh, Buffalo, and Denver—this was simply deleted by a copy editor.

Furthermore, nearly everyone, including the press, has generally assumed that the auditions are private. The preliminaries are, but the finals are held in the ostentatious "privacy" of either Carnegie or Town Hall, where anyone sufficiently interested is welcome to walk in and listen. It often amuses me—as I hear the anguished cries of all those who can't buy seats for love or money—to recall the day Van played on and on and free for nothing before some thirty people in the hall; and that number included all the eliminated contestants.

Ah well, that's always the way. Or, perhaps more accurately, that *was* always the way, for now heartening signs are around which indicate a healthier climate of interest in accomplishment itself, and we'll come to them presently.

On that Sunday afternoon of November 14, 1954, when Van played his award engagement with the Philharmonic at Carnegie Hall, Mrs. Leventritt stayed backstage. During intermission he asked her to look out through the peephole into the auditorium. "Honey," he said, "do you see all those people down front? They're up here from Texas, every one of 'em. Just as soon as this is over, I'm bringing them all

64

over to your house, so you'd best go home and start to get ready!"

Her inborn Alabaman hospitality instantly aroused, Mrs. Leventritt hurried home to alert her household; and sure enough, in due course her bell rang and in trooped Van with his retinue of genial giants, accompanied by their ladies. Presenting his hostess with a mammoth basket of red roses he had somehow managed to pick up along the way, Van went straight to the piano and began to play the Schumann-Liszt "*Widmung*," singing with feeling: "*Du meine Seele, du mein Herz.*" It was his characteristic way of saying, "I thank you. I love you."

Among the sharpest observers at Carnegie Hall that afternoon had been Schuyler Chapin, then the Midwest representative of Columbia Artists Management, Inc., and Mrs. Chapin, the former Betty Steinway. Both had heard Van play at Juilliard and were familiar with his "exciting talent and fantastic gift." But never having heard him before in front of a large audience, they were unprepared for the emotional warmth of the listeners' response, flabbergasted to notice the many who rose to acclaim him. As they stood up with the others, clamoring for the boy to come out and take his fifth curtain call, then his sixth, and his seventh, they realized that Van had, in addition to his musicianship, the even rarer quality of exciting his audience. Chapin thought it was a characteristic that would come through strikingly on TV, if given the chance.

By now Van had signed the contract that had lain for so long on Bill Judd's Jacobean desk. So, on behalf of CAMI, Chapin called up Skitch Henderson, music director of Steve Allen's "Tonight" show, among the first commercial network programs to telecast an occasional spot of serious music, untainted by horseplay or gimmicks. Skitch went to hear Van play at the home of Chapin's mother-in-law, Mrs. Theodore Steinway, and came away convinced. Then he tried to promote "Vaniel," as he calls him, with the powers that be.

The resistance was formidable. Bad enough, they argued, to present a longhair at all, but at least his name should be Leonard Bernstein or Isaac Stern or something. Who ever heard of this Van What's-his-name? Or, for that matter, what kind of a deal is this Leventritt Award?

But Skitch, as Chapin says, "really lit the fire and kept it crackling." Van appeared on the "Tonight" show on January 19, 1955, playing the Ravel Toccata and a Chopin étude over seventy-five stations and to an audience of three or four million people. "In the whole history of the 'Tonight' show," Skitch Henderson asserts, "that was one of the four of five peak nights that stand out in memory. Vaniel was terrific. In the language of show biz, he just broke it up!"

The switchboard blossomed with telephone calls; and one, long-distance, was a firm bid for an engagement. The Glee Club of the Baltimore & Ohio railroad employees wanted the new boy to play for them the following May. Telegrams, letters piled into the mail room. When Chapin left for the Midwest to start booking for the following season he was asked everywhere he went about "that extraordinary guy with the hair we saw on TV." He booked about ten concerts for Van which were directly in response to the TV exposure. Meanwhile, Steve Allen, the star of the show, said: "Let's have this guy back."

The guy was back in April for another appearance. But—again in the language of show biz—this time "he died." What was the trouble? The post-mortem consensus blamed a number of factors. One was a hilarious comedy routine which put the huge audience in the wrong mood to listen to classical music; and the second was the repertoire, an ill-advised one for the time and place: a short piece by Medtner followed by a long, introspective work by Chopin.

More than three years were to pass before Vaniel appeared on TV again. On the platform, however, he was to chalk up dozens of artistic triumphs, one more impressive than the other.

The first year after Leventritt (1955–56) he played thirty engagements, including reappearances with the symphony orchestras of Cleveland, Denver, and Buffalo. Such reappearances are rare with the big orchestras, regardless of the extent of the artist's success. Van was recalled to Cleveland for three repeats that season alone.

In addition to nine Community Concerts, he performed with the symphonies of Indianapolis, Houston, Detroit, Montreal; of Canton, Ohio, and South Bend, Indiana. The last engagement was due to Chapin's dropping to his knees before Mrs. Ernest Morris, who books the South Bend series, clasping his hands together in mock petition, and imploring her to give his new pianist a chance. *Please,* kind lady, try him just once——

"Why?" she asked, laughing.

Because, Chapin promised, the young artist would not only deliver a terrific performance but would also establish a rapport with his audience which no one would ever forget. If she engaged him once, he guaranteed that her subscribers would certainly want him again.

Mrs. Morris bought; and true to Chapin's prediction, South Bend became a regular stop on Van's future itinerary. It was not until the 1958 season that management there

67

thought a "new face" was in order; and, ironically, that was the year Van became *the* new face, the shiniest of them all.

Van's gross income the first year after Leventritt was about $19,000. His fee varied, of course, with the town and situation. "He was the first American pianist for whom we tried to get $1000 a performance from the start," Bill Judd says, "and we got it in quite a few places." Sometimes the price was $300 or $400.

Professional expenses, however—managerial commissions, publicity, pictures, traveling expenses, and the costs of living on the road—take a formidable bite out of an artist's gross earnings. After such expenses, plus taxes, it is likely that Van averaged something around $150 a week to live on. Not an impressive wage for a stage electrician, perhaps, but an excellent income for any concert artist who is not a box-office magnet like Rubinstein or Heifetz or Tebaldi.

If the winning of the Leventritt was the first "giant step" in Van's public career, now the earning of money led to personal as well as financial independence. He moved from the Spicer's Claremont Avenue apartment down to West 57th Street, right in the heart of New York's "Music Row." For the first time the artist as young man was keeping bachelor quarters and getting a huge kick out of furnishing his three-room studio-apartment.

One-third of his pale gray living room was taken up by his inseparable companion—the graceful, big Steinway. An entire wall was dominated by an in-a-bed sofa, in case his parents should come up for a visit. But the chairs, tables, dressers, lamps . . . all reflected the personal taste which he now was developing.

Between concerts he went to museums and galleries and fascinating shops. At the museum of the Frick Collection, packed with treasures, he discovered a natural affinity for the romantic elegance of the great French periods. Most of the pieces he picked up in the auction rooms were either Louis XVI or Empire, and some of his acquisitions were frankly bargains. Everything showed fine discrimination—a fruit-wood bureau with large, brass handles; a Directoire bench for the long, narrow hallway, where Hogarth prints embellished the wall; a low, marble-topped table. Antique mirrors, stacked against the fireplace, blocked out the garish hardness of painted red brick. But Chinese red was used from floor to ceiling in the tiny kitchenette, to suggest the inside of a bright, lacquered box.

The bedroom, too, was not very spacious. It contained a wide double bed, an antique dresser, a handsome pewter samovar made into a lamp, and red velvet hangings. On the night-stand by the pillow—his well-thumbed Bible.

When the phone was installed Van asked the telephone company for an extra-long cord. Since he is equally beset by two conflicting urges, one to be all alone and the other never to be alone if he can possibly find company, a telephone is as necessary to him as a pair of ears. With it he effects a compromise: solitude in actuality . . . but with someone to talk to.

The lovely Nola Rhodes, who, with her husband Ted, is one of Van's closest friends from Calvary Church, got a call from him one morning and sat chatting for the better part of an hour on the phone. Eventually she began to suspect something besides conversation was going on at the other end of the line.

"What *are* you doing, Van?" she inquired.

"Putting my shoes on," he told her cheerfully. And only then did she learn that, since calling her up, he had cooked his breakfast, eaten it, got himself dressed, and was ready to go out—all without once dropping the receiver cradled under his chin! Since he does the same sort of thing long-distance his telephone bills are always astronomical.

Personal friends such as the Rhodeses or Spicers, who have seen Van close-up over a period of years, say they have never known him to evade facing up to the truth, whether it hurts him or—with regret—hurts somebody else. Nor have they ever heard him use profanity, no matter what the provocation.

The story is told that in Buffalo, in the midst of a concerto, one of the pedals came off the piano. Josef Krips, the conductor, did not react to this interruption of his performance with what could be exactly called a nerveless stoicism or philosophic calm. To put it bluntly, he plain blew his stack. The air about his podium was on the verge of turning a rich sulphuric blue when Van walked over, took the maestro's arm, and led him courteously but resolutely off to a dressing room. "Let us pray," Van said quietly, bowing his head. The astonished maestro, bound by simple respect and civility to do the same thing, began to simmer down. By the time the pedal was repaired tempers were restored, and the concert could resume in an atmosphere of serenity.

This incident, misunderstood by some sections of the press, had Van pulling Krips to his knees before the concert began and intoning: "God give us His grace and power to make good music together."

"It makes me sound like a fool!" Van fumed when he read it, always cut to the quick by any story that seems to expose his religion to ridicule. Pious he is and quite unashamed of it; but sanctimonious, never.

In fact, members of the choir at Calvary consistently accuse him of keeping them laughing all through rehearsals with skylarking pranks. And Gleason Frye, the choral director for whom Van served intermittently as organist, has an indelible picture in his memory of the afternoon Van could not resist "ragging" some of the real-gone old gospel hymns, which may be good theology but which are a trial to musicians. "He was all over the keyboard," as Gleason Frye describes it, "up, down, rolling his eyes and giving out with these terrible tremolos and horribly lush chords—when the door opens suddenly, and there stands the minister!" Without missing a lick Van segued gracefully into his most circumspect Sunday-morning treatment, looking for all the world like St. Cecilia at the organ.

In the summer of 1956, Mrs. Leventritt arranged a scholarship for him at the school in Marlboro, Vermont, headed by Rudolf Serkin. Van loved the Serkins, and they loved him; but the school is mainly for chamber-music players and auditors, and it soon became evident to everyone that this was not his bailiwick.

Moreover, in mid-July he received a request to play the Rachmaninoff Concerto No. 2 in C Minor on August 4 with the Cleveland Summer Orchestra. He had played the Third Rachmaninoff many times but never the Second; nevertheless, he wired an acceptance, then rushed back to New York to pick up the score. "I've got just two weeks to learn it," he told Gleason Frye, immediately plunking himself down at the keyboard to explore his way through his own part, then the orchestra's part, then his own part again, humming and singing the whole thing as he went. "And," says Gleason Frye, with the ear of a choral director, "always on key."

Back to Vermont again, and incessantly occupied with the new score—to the neglect, necessarily, of his other

Marlboro projects. But no amount of work packed into a short period, no facility to learn quickly, can supplant the considered contemplation and experience required to achieve artistic wholeness, creative or re-creative.

When Van appeared in Cleveland the concert was covered for the *Plain Dealer* on August 5 by Rena C. Holtkamp:

> A Texas-sized helping of Rachmaninoff was served up at the Cleveland Summer Orchestra's pop concert in Public Hall last night by Louis Lane, Texas-born conductor, assisted by tall Van Cliburn, piano soloist who grew up in Texas.
>
> Cliburn is a favorite pianist here . . . Last night, for an audience of 3,500, he played the most popular and expansive of all Rachmaninoff's big works (the Second Piano Concerto in C minor). Cliburn's playing has always been highly musical and forceful, and this was no exception . . . and the durable work was warmly received.
>
> For an encore, Cliburn played . . . "Toccata" by Ravel.

In this "Cliburn town" and for this resplendent piece anything less than a thunderous reaction suggests that this time Van did not make the welkin ring. Truth to tell, Van himself felt lukewarm about the work and to date has not played it since.

Returning to Marlboro for what was left of the summer, Van did some work on a Mozart concerto and on the Dvořák Piano Quintet, for which he felt an especial affinity; but when the 'cellist fell ill and the scheduled performance of that piece was canceled he was ready to leave. The truth is that Van has always been "a born flaming virtuoso," as I have often described him, and his solo bigness simply would not dovetail with the minute and delicate balances of adjustment needed for ensemble work. Instinctively he knew this and turned, as he always has turned, to what offered the greatest fulfillment to his individual genius. "Van Cliburn," a musicologist observed, "is more the product of intuition than tuition."

This season of 1955–56, taken all in all, was Van's biggest year: the beginning, many would have said, of a progressively happy and spiraling career. He was well on his way now, a young man who just about had it "made."

Then, within reach of his goal, he stepped into a series of those booby traps that bestrew the path of mortals, as though to remind us that the last word is not ours. The first, utterly beyond one's reckoning, was even more frightening than a threat to his career. Who could have foreseen that his childhood regime, the specialization in music to the exclusion of all else, would nearly cost him his life?

Early that summer he was invited by the Chapins to spend a weekend at the Steinway place in Plymouth, Massachusetts. Soon after arrival the Chapin children wanted "Uncle Moving Van" and the rest of the family to go for a dip in the water. Everyone got into swim suits and went out to the dock, where Chapin issued the usual warning, always sounded to visitors, to beware of the submerged shelf that dropped away suddenly, a few feet from shore. He plunged in and started swimming, while Van fooled around in shallow water with the kids.

"The first thing I knew," Chapin relates, "is that I missed Van. Then I saw his head pop up and his arms thrashing wildly. I thought he was fooling. But down he went again, and it seemed forever before his head reappeared. Then it hit me like a bolt from left field—he was *drowning!*"

Yelling at his wife, who was just coming out of the house, to dive in after him, Chapin struck out to reach Van and caught him just as the bushy mane was vanishing beneath the surface for the third time. Together, he and Betty pushed and propelled their soggy guest to shore and pummeled the water out of his lungs.

"Why didn't you *tell* us you couldn't swim?" Chapin demanded explosively, when Van had stopped strangling. But their curious friend would only shake his head apologetically; and as soon as he was able to stand he waded back into the water. "I'm going to stay right here till I get used to it!" he declared, hanging onto the dock. And stay there he did, though he was quaking in the knees and covered with goose bumps.

Gleason Frye tells the rest of the story:

"When Van came back to New York he told me how close he had come to drowning. He blamed the whole thing on the fact that he had never had any sort of physical training, and he envied me because, though I was a musician too, I had worked for five summers as a lifeguard and swimming instructor. He said his whole life had been 'music, music, music'; he'd give anything if he could overcome his fear of water and just learn to swim. I said I'd be willing to teach him if he was that serious about it. He said, 'It's a deal.'"

Frye had a job that occupied him all day, and Van was usually busy at night. The only time they could get together was early in the morning, before Frye went to work. So at 6 A.M., sleepy-eyed but determined, they would travel over to Brooklyn by subway and get in an hour's lesson in the big pool at the Hotel St. George.

"I've never seen anyone so scared of water in my life," Frye says, "and I've never seen anyone turn that shade of white. Here was this great hulk of a guy, completely petrified in water that came only up to his knees! My heart really bled for him. But he kept saying, 'I'm going to get over this if it's the last thing I ever do in my life.' And he finally did. In a month's time he could go across the pool in only one breath. The pity of it is, of course, that with his physique and co-ordination he always had the makings of a first-class swimmer."

The next time Van saw Schuyler Chapin was when they met at someone's recital. They talked in the lobby until the bell-ringing signaled the end of intermission, then they started back for their separate seats. Just before they parted Van glanced over his shoulder. "Oh, by the way," he said casually, "I can swim now."

No explanation. Just a big, self-satisfied, 18-carat grin.

6

Molto Rallentando

In Italian, the melodious language of musical terms, *molto rallentando* expresses a slackening of speed, going steadily slower and slower.

It describes what now began to happen to Van, and it has foreboded the decay of many a promising career. Van's first concert season had yielded eighteen engagements. The second, thirty. The deceleration began in the third season, when he was booked for twenty-three; yet still among them were some excellent dates, including five orchestral appearances in Detroit, Cleveland, South Bend, Shreveport, and Dallas. Of the remaining engagements, all but two were recitals in tiny towns scattered across the landscape from New Brunswick to Arizona.

The fourth season of 1957–58 started in earnest to stack up as a long, lean haul except for faithful Cleveland, which invited him back for a concerto date in July. The prospects after that were three October recitals for Community Concerts in McAllen and Graham, Texas, and in Natchitoches,

Louisiana; a blank for three months; then two more recitals in Norwalk, Ohio, and in Coldwater, Michigan. Beyond that, nothing at all.

Meanwhile, the 1958–59 bookings were under way. But though the itinerary was shaping up somewhat less grimly and included one low-fee but high-prestige date with the New York Philharmonic, it looked suspiciously like the handwriting on the wall to the thoroughly disenchanted Van Cliburn.

What was happening?

Nothing new. Nothing at all unusual which had not previously happened to the cream of American musicians of our generation, one after the other.

To understand the shocking fact even dimly, one must inure oneself to some of the dour realities of the concert world. Without a management the soloist cannot function except on a semiprofessional basis. About 90 per cent of all the artists who appear in this country have been booked for a great many years now by two concert agencies whose networks sprawl across the continent: Columbia Artists Management, Inc., and National Artists Corporation, which together control about 90 per cent of all available concert engagements. Both of these chains own affiliates that service some twelve hundred cities through an organized-audience plan. CAMI's affiliate, Community Concerts, commands some 850 towns. NAC's counterpart, Civic Music Association, commands the rest.

Undeniably, the system provides cultural benefits to communities, expanded opportunities for artists to perform, and a sound economic scheme that enables a lot of people to buy a lot of entertainment. The concept itself is admirable; but, as I remarked in *Speaking of Pianists,* the same could be said about the wheel until it was attached to a cannon. For the mechanism of this concept, unfortunately, has a built-in dead end for most artists.

The average town raises enough money to contract for a series of four or five concerts annually. Subscribers are attracted by one Big-Name orchestra or soloist who will pull in the public and a deservedly whopping fee, leaving a few hundred dollars in the treasury for each remaining "filler" soloist or group.

Variety is the spice of this plan and not only because of the customers' limited opportunities to hear and to meet artists: re-engagements are discouraged, regardless of the success of the filler artist, also in order to preserve the economics of the plan. Any artist who is allowed to build a public—no matter how modest—any public that could become *his* public, might impede the assembly-line operation. Requests for his reappearance may cause embarrassment when management prefers to use the date otherwise; building a loyal following permits an artist to acquire bargaining power. It gives him "ideas," and he may even ask for a well-merited fee hike, which would make him harder and harder to sell and within the budget of fewer and fewer towns.

Of course, in addition to Community or Civic concerts there are also other outlets known to the trade as "straight sales," which include orchestral dates, college series, and recital courses presented by local impresarios. However, such engagements are mainly available to those artists with large reputations or forceful personal representation. Van had quite a few of them during his first two seasons, principally orchestral dates, most of which are traceable to the Leventritt prize. After that, they just dried up.

In the concert business of the United States there is room

at the top, which the filler artist can rarely reach from his pigeonhole, and at the bottom, from which escape is almost impossible. In between is No Man's Land. And that is precisely the situation that the majority of our finest pianists have had to face.

And where are they, these first-rate people? Most of them are no place. A few of the luckiest are just where Cliburn now begins to find himself in our narrative. They have managers. They play some prestige dates. Their names are no larger than their fees. They are struggling to hold an artistic position they have fully earned, hoping for the fundamental rights that belong to all other workers: the chance to do their work, to earn a decent living from it, to develop in it, and to anticipate recognition and advancement from a job honestly and well performed. With few exceptions it has been a quite hopeless hope because of America's indifference to the quality or fate of its artists, because of managerial apathy and/or helplessness in merchandising excellence without a gimmick.

When the little names run their due course, there are plenty of others to replace them, all begging for the chance. The chance for what? Ask Van Cliburn, who had to get out from under in order not to be buried alive.

From here in it is easy to see what happened and why. Sooner or later comes the zero hour, the time when the young artist finds he has played all or most of the towns available and suddenly awakens to discover that his dates have evaporated. Some of the more "fortunate" ones are invited to stay on if they can form their own ensembles or will become anonymous members of "group-attractions," an ever increasing trend that has further jeopardized the soloist. The majority call it a day and vanish from the concert scene to find teaching jobs or to quit music entirely.

Still others, when their personal lives permit, go abroad in search of some opportunity to do their work. That's exactly what Van had decided to do, and what Bill Judd encouraged him to do, for it was clear that Van was headed for "the treatment," in defiance of his management's best efforts.

Ironically, it was all the more difficult for Van to swallow because of these efforts, which inaugurated so auspicious a beginning. Many of Van's colleagues were nowhere, and he knew it. They had also won prizes, and some had also won the chance to make their debuts with major orchestras. But how many had ever been sought out and courted by management . . . and by such a management? Virtually none, among our native artists. Most others, hat in hand and a fistful of glowing notices in the other, pleaded for contracts, offering to play anywhere at any price, expecting nothing further. They were rarely disappointed and still more rarely regarded as anything but expendable products, no matter how brilliantly they delivered when they got the chance.

Van, on the other hand, was carefully nurtured. His first tours and first earnings were phenomenal, largely due to Judd's and Chapin's interest and efforts and to their conviction that Van's particular qualities would finally reward their exertions and make a long-range plan work.

But even this trio couldn't beat the system, not to mention the national apathy toward our art and our artists.

For one of those artists the empty months of idleness in 1957 constituted the "dark night of the soul." His shining young talent was rusting, his joyous self-confidence corroding. He knew the bitterest of all experiences, the enforced disuse of a natural function about which his entire being revolved and without which he might be said to have no existence at all. He vegetated and despaired.

All of us are manic to some degree, each with his up-in-the-sky and down-in-the-dumps moments, but the necessarily supersensitive responses of the artistic temperament make for wider and more frequent swings. And when bread and butter or professional life and death are at stake, the danger of something cracking within is very real and very understandable.

Van became distraught and confused. Trying to analyze his problem, hoping to find some thread to lead him out of his bewilderment, he spent hours with friends on the phone. He grew so peaked and pale from moping about the apartment that Nola Rhodes would coax him over to Riverside Drive for a little air and sun. They'd find a place down near the river's edge, as secluded as possible, and he would peel off his shirt. "Ugh, I look so white!" he'd say, wrinkling his nose at the sight of his pale hide. Then, as they watched the boats go by, he and Nola would talk about what was happening to him and his work. Once, when a gleaming cabin cruiser glided up the channel, his eyes followed her longingly. "I want a boat like that!" he exclaimed, with a flash of his old eagerness. "Oh, Nola, I seem to want *everything*. I want to travel, I want to help my parents, I want to be a really great artist, I want to go everywhere, see everything, know everybody! And here I am—look at me. Going nowhere, fast!"

"I'd talk to Van as I would to a younger brother," Mrs. Rhodes says in reconstructing this period. "I used to say to him, 'Van, if you'll practice and have faith I predict to you right now that you'll have all those things you want, and a lot more besides. You have the talent to get to the top, and you have the personality, too.'"

Usually this pep talk worked. Van never wanted sympathy. He just wanted to be bucked up. "Oh, you inspire me!" he would cry, with a new burst of energy. "Come on, let's go —I have to get home and practice."

When there were concerts to play the keyboard held a compelling fascination and he would work tirelessly for hours. But with no engagement on the immediate horizon he was inclined to write practice off as pointless drudgery. He would arrange walking dates, movie dates, concert dates, anything to find diversion. Mother Cliburn had a sixth sense about these matters, and almost as soon as Van eased up on his work she would call his friends long-distance from Texas: "Please see that Van practices."

Van's dwindling earnings were the least of his worries. Mere money was expendable. While in Montreal his observant eye was caught by a chic chapeau in a window, a Jacques Fath copy, and he promptly bought it for his mother. On his own clothes he hardly spent anything.

His taste in food was fortunately flexible. He still ate a few times a week in smart New York restaurants, courtesy of friends who appreciated his company. At other times, when he dined alone, he would drop in at the Carnegie Hall Tavern, where the friendly waiters knew of old that he had a weakness for pot roast. They also knew, with that extrasensory perception which waiters have for regular patrons, that he could no longer afford it. They would advise him to order the pot roast sandwich at half the price. "It's just the same," they'd say, and would see to it that it was—a full order of pot roast camouflaged between two slices of rye.

Van never went hungry. It's even unlikely that he ever

skipped a meal except when practice sessions blotted out time, and such intensive sessions were growing more and more infrequent. Between periods of renewed vigor, each one more short-lived than the last, Van would plunge again to become abidingly, disturbingly unhappy, and his mother's time-honored maxims, which had guided him all his life, were often on his lips:

You can't just sit on the tracks and pray. That won't stop the train.

Cast thy bread upon the waters.

In Van's book this last precept has always been honored by much more than lip service. Both before and after Moscow a number of music students and professionals have told of timely handouts in moments of need, received from a helping hand that was not necessarily full itself. Such spontaneous gestures are in the tradition of art, born of the camaraderie with which struggling poets and painters and musicians have always tried to relieve each other's privations. Give and take, in a literal sense. Everyone is familiar with it, in or out of the art world. What may puzzle those brought up to live prudently within one's means is that in the spring of 1957, facing an economic vacuum, Van elected to make his costliest present to date. Impulsive it may have been, at least in conception; but there was never any later indication of a second's regret.

Calvary Church broadcast its service each Sunday over WMGM. On this particular occasion Van was at the console for a presentation of Mozart's Requiem Mass, when suddenly the big pipe organ lost its breath entirely and wheezed to a stop. Gleason Frye, conducting the choir, carried on with the voices minus the instrumental underpinning; and while listeners at home undoubtedly wondered what on earth was going on Van scrambled down from the organ loft and supported the work to its conclusion on the patriarchal piano.

It was then that he decided Calvary Baptist Church must have a decent piano in its organ loft, immediately at hand. He went out and bought one, a brand-new Steinway. Even allowing for the discount given to concert artists, it cost easily as much as the Cadillac convertible he never could afford and after which he always hungered. Van borrowed the money from a bank and settled down to a long stretch of monthly installments.

Meantime, his health began to be a cause for concern. He suffered chronically from "performer's stomach," which thrived on his worry and depression. And he had always had a deviated septum which tended to become ulcerated from head colds or sinus. One night that spring he telephoned friends in the middle of the night to report that blood had been running from his nose for hours and that he could not seem to stanch it. The experience was frightening.

Other personal problems clouded the horizon. At the age of twenty-one, he had received a two-year deferment on army training, so he could finish at Juilliard. The two years would be up in September, and he must report for induction. Being outspoken Van, he made no secret that this was impending and talked of it freely, even on tour. His management took a dim view of such inexpedient candor and wished he would play his cards a little closer to the vest. Even now, they are convinced that one of the major reasons for his paucity of advance bookings for 1958–59 was that, during the period when such engagements were being scheduled, so many were so certain that Van would be in training with a Springfield instead of a Steinway.

That was my own belief, for around that time I invited him to appear in a series of radio recitals over WQXR, and he told me he did not "dare to accept" because of his uncertain military status. He seemed disheartened about everything, and there are indications that this mental and emotional slump affected his playing. Here and there comments filtered back to management of casual performances. However, the report from the next town might show that he had not only picked himself up but had left them spellbound.

The one bright spot for the year seemed to be the July 20 date with the Cleveland Summer Orchestra. Mr. and Mrs. Cliburn decided to drive up from Texas for that event, and the family was reunited at a Cleveland hotel. It was a happy occasion for all of them. But the happiness was of brief duration. Just before the concert, and while Mrs. Cliburn was changing her clothes, she slipped and went over backward, striking the floor with her back. The fall was a heavy one, and Van and his father, both in a state of alarm, called the house doctor. Mrs. Cliburn insisted, however, that she was not going to miss the performance; so after taking some tablets for the pain she went along to the concert—an especially fine one, from all reports.

The next morning they all piled into the family Buick and headed for New York. By this time Mrs. Cliburn was in agony but still thought she had only a wrench or sprain which would get better by itself in a number of days. When they arrived in Manhattan she was able to rest in bed during the day but got up at night to go to Madison Square Garden and occupy Van's private box at Billy Graham's giant evangelist meeting. The revival had been in full swing for weeks, and Van had often, as a member of the choir, helped to uphold the bass section on such perennials as

"Blessed Assurance," "I Love to Tell the Story," and "Wonderful Words of Life." Ethel Waters was also around, rendering stalwart service to the alto section. The evangelist had assigned Van a box for his personal use early in the campaign. Here Van kept spiritual open house, as it were, throughout Graham's engagement. Among his guests were many young musicians. From Juilliard he brought John Browning, the 1955 Leventritt winner, and his old pals from Texas, Jimmy Mathis and Jeaneane Dowis.

Meanwhile, after a long week of suffering and hoping for the best Mrs. Cliburn agreed to visit a doctor and to have her back X-rayed. The pictures showed a broken vertebra and also that the accident had been a very narrow escape. Just a fraction nearer the spinal column and she might never have walked again. Skillful treatment was immediately required. Into Doctors Hospital she went, to lie in one position for the next six weeks.

This was just about the end. Illness costs money, but hospitals can be murder. For the first time Van really understood the meaning of financial pressure. With an empty calendar stretching before him, he decided to lock the door of his apartment, at least for the time being, and go back to Kilgore. His father was able to raise a loan at the local bank to take care of medical expenses, but there remained the matter of his mother's pupils. She still had forty-odd, now left without a teacher, and he might as well fill in the gap till his army number came up. But the last thing he did before leaving New York was to clean out his bank account and put down several months in advance on the church piano so that Calvary would not be "stuck" with the payments. As for the future, he could use his army pay to meet the installments.

Six weeks in Kilgore was something of a tonic. Van has always liked kids. With his habitual unawareness of the clock, even though payment was fixed on an hourly basis, he would become fascinated with a lesson, continue until his young pupil reminded him, "My time's way over. Please may I go now?" And when the tiny Lutheran church sent over to see if Mrs. Cliburn had a pupil who could play at their services Van went himself. All the time he was in Kilgore he accompanied their hymns on a small Estey organ.

Came the day he was summoned to the nearest induction center in Longview, Texas. Everything got under way serenely, but before the day was over his nose began to bleed. It bled on and on, the army medics being no more successful in shutting the thing off than Van had been himself. Examination quickly disclosed the condition of the septum—long-standing, chronic. He was out before he was in. Classification, 4-F.

With this his luck changed. Unsuspected, powerful currents were beginning to stir that would overtake him, seize him, and carry him on headlong. One of these currents had to do, quite incredibly, with mankind's long dream of conquering space. On a never-to-be-forgotten morning in early October of '57, Americans woke up to the lacerating news that, while they slept, something called a sputnik had been rocketed skyward and sent into orbit by the insidious Russians. An insupportable thought: "they" were the first to conquer outer space! Soon "they" sent up a dog to whirl over our heads, which seemed rubbing it in. Americans, smoldering, were forced to sit tight for five interminable months before they were able to see their own Vanguard's red glare pierce the dawn's early light—and we, as a nation, are not accustomed to that kind of waiting. A lot of people were dying to beat the Russkies at something, at anything, to even things up; if only at a game of chess—or Russian bank.

"Is he lucky?" Napoleon would ask before appointing a general. Luck, from now on, could have been Van Cliburn's alias. To be sure, he did not make the Cold War and would have preferred to do without it. Yet *it* made *him*, in the sense that it provided a nuclear charge to those three classic ingredients: the right man at the right time in the right place.

At this particular moment in history the rightest place in the whole wide world for the right man to be, was precisely where Van was going. Although as yet he didn't know it.

> There is a tide in the affairs of men,
> Which, taken at the flood, leads on to fortune—

The tide of the Cliburn career was just coming in.

7

Russian Roulette

Success is a game of roulette. Take it from a man
who has played it a lot. One day a city or a nation
doesn't know you're alive. The next day they're
killing themselves to get near you.

ARTUR RUBINSTEIN

As I opened the door to my office one November morning,
I heard the telephone ringing and, over the loudspeaker, one
of our WQXR announcers broadcasting the hourly news
bulletin of *The New York Times*: "In the Security Council
of the United Nations yesterday the Russian delegate de-
nounced the United States for its——" I turned it off to
answer the phone. It was from Rosina Lhevinne. I sat down
to chat without the slightest inkling that I had actually
taken a ringside seat for an impending drama. She came
right to the point:

"Abram, what would you think of Van's going to Moscow
for the Tchaikovsky Competition?"

I knew what *that* meant. Van's career evidently needed a shot in the arm . . . and urgently enough to risk a return to the competitive arena. It was not too unexpected, but I filled my pipe to gain time to formulate and frame my answer.

"Why not?" I finally said. "What has Van got to lose?"—which forever will remain the understatement of my entire life.

"Now," Madame said, "we have to find the money to get him over there."

It was only much later, when the fabulous jigsaw puzzle was pieced together, that anyone seemed to get a coherent picture of exactly how the whole adventure came about.

Mme. Lhevinne recounts:

"In the fall of 1957 my pupil, Olegna Fuschi, went down to Brazil to take part in a contest. While there, a Russian member of the jury, Pavel Seribriakov, handed her a brochure describing the first Tchaikovsky International Piano and Violin Festival to be held in Moscow during March and April."

Miss Fuschi says: "After I returned I brought the brochure along to my next lesson, although I myself had no intention of going into another contest. Madame read the brochure, then, holding it in her hand, she went to the window and looked out, staring. Suddenly I heard her say very softly, half to herself, 'Van.'"

Mme. Lhevinne then dictated a letter to be sent off to Van. Being a Russian herself, she reminded him, and a graduate of the Moscow Conservatory, she knew the Russian taste well. She was certain that his big, sweeping approach and romantic manner of playing would appeal to them strongly. "I promise, they will love you."

Van, in Texas, was slow to catch fire. He talked it over with his parents and with others seriously concerned with his future. In the twelfth year of the Cold War, there were many people who would have expressed the same doubt which he got from all sides: Yes, but no matter how well you play, will the Soviets let an *American* win?

He wrote back, expressing his truly deep gratitude to Mme. Lhevinne for thinking of him, but after consideration he had decided against it.

Meantime, of course, other announcements of the Tchaikovsky Competition had been received in New York, and more than one interested person, remembering how often Van had won over here with the Tchaikovsky First, thought of him as a natural contender, perhaps even a natural winner. The late Alexander Greiner, head of Steinway's Concerts and Artists department, kept in close touch with the situation from the beginning and was a charter member of the "Van to Moscow" movement.

Others who soon appeared in the supporting faction were William Schuman and Mark Schubart of Juilliard. When Mme. Lhevinne first approached the former on the proposition of sending Van to Russia he asked only, "Are you sure he's the right one?"

"He is, from my classes," Mme. Lhevinne answered. "And besides, I feel he would make a wonderful representative of America in Moscow. He has the personality as well as the talent."

With Juilliard's blessing, Mme. Lhevinne again wrote to Texas. This time she presented her arguments in Wilsonian fashion, carefully marshaled into tabulated points:

Point 1: You will have to work with great intensity,

and this will be good for you, regardless of the contest.

Point 2: You will have to learn a great deal of new material.

Point 3: You will meet the elite of the young pianists from other parts of the world.

Point 4: Last, but not least—I believe you will win.

Down in Texas, the Alamo wavered. He still thought he shouldn't go, Van responded, but he would be in New York around the first of November, and he would come to see her and discuss it.

Early in November Van came to dinner at Mme. Lhevinne's apartment. Miss Fuschi was staying there at the time, and they all three sat around studying the brochure of the contest and discussing his chances. The prize money offered—25,000 rubles, or $6,250 at the official rate of exchange—did not tempt Van nearly so much as the Tchaikovsky Gold Medal.

At the impressionable age of twelve he had read, back in Kilgore, how his hero Rachmaninoff had received the Great Gold Medal at the Moscow Conservatory, and this had plunged him for weeks into a rosy syndrome of Walter Mitty daydreams. In the spring of '57 the half-forgotten fantasy had been revived, unexpectedly, by a chance encounter with some psychic, who prophesied that within a twelvemonth he would make a journey to "an agrarian country" where he would win a gold medal. Who among us is so free of superstition as not to cock a half-hopeful ear in the direction of Macbeth's voices, especially when our luck is running low? Van did not "believe," exactly. Yet he remembered, and this may have provided just the extra pinch of stardust that threw the balance on the scales.

The competitive spirit in Van, always strong from earliest childhood, once again began to flare at the challenge. Off he would go—possibly, maybe. Soon he and Mme. Lhevinne were talking about the repertoire he would have to prepare, *if*, and how long it would take to master the program.

Still there were powerful, negative voices. "But you can't *do* that, Rosina!" Bill Judd cried, horrified. Not only was he appalled at the thought of another contest, but he had also lined up that European tour for Van in the spring. However, since this was of the self-financed variety its cancellation would be merely a matter of routine. The strongest deterrent was still the political mistrust that now rose in a crescendo of ominous warnings: "Don't go. Don't go! An American will *never* be permitted to win."

Rosina Lhevinne shrugged her shoulders at this. Whether or not the Soviets "permitted" an American to win—and who could know the answer to that one?—the hard work involved in preparation, the stimulus to be derived, would be ample rewards in themselves. If Van eventually decided for any reason that he wanted to withdraw he could cancel up to the last moment. But he must register now.

So the application was made out and sent in. Van had one foot at least on the bank of the Rubicon.

Mark Schubart, on behalf of Juilliard, had already gone through channels to sound out the State Department's attitude, as of that date, toward the participation of Americans in competitions behind the Iron Curtain. He was given to understand that the State Department favored such participation and would place no restrictions on travel. "At the same time," Schubart says, "I was informed that no funds were available to take care of transportation to Moscow." Since the U.S.S.R. was prepared to pay contestants' expenses within the Soviet Union, as well as return fare, all that was needed was the wherewithal for the journey across.

Mr. Greiner gave me a ring. "We don't have the setup for this sort of thing at Steinway's," he said regretfully. "But Van simply must go, somehow. Rosina told me you agree. I'm taking him to lunch today to talk things over." Much later Van was to recall how much he owed to Greiner's encouragement. "He took me to lunch three times, and in his inimitable fashion said: 'Dear Van, I beg of you, *please* go. You must.' He seemed so confident I would win that he had a great deal to do with making up my mind."

Mark Schubart was pushing ahead on the financial angle —not for Van especially, but for whatever artists might finally emerge as the United States' entries. He approached the Institute of International Education and from there was referred to César Saerchinger at the foundation named for Martha Baird Rockefeller, herself at one time a professional pianist. It was this foundation's Aid to Music Program which came to the rescue, agreeing to provide traveling expenses for those contestants who would go from here. Having determined that America's contenders would not have to swim the Atlantic, Mark Schubart served written notice to the Institute: "At this point I should like to bow out of this matter, since I have one, and possibly two, candidates to recommend and therefore am something of an interested party." He urged, however, that the contestants be selected on an invitational basis only and without publicity, "since our only hope to be well represented in the Tchaikovsky Competition devolves upon our being able to send to Moscow not students, but young professionals, preferably with a good deal of concert experience. This caliber of young artist would undoubtedly not wish to participate in a competition just to take part in a competition. Certainly there can be only one criterion in deciding upon contestants—namely, ability to perform."

In due course several names were submitted as possibilities. Most of them said no, *thanks*. But it was known that Daniel Pollack of Los Angeles, another Lhevinne pupil and Juilliard product, was planning to enter the lists, as were pianists Norman Shetler and Jerome Lowenthal. All three were already in Europe, furthering their studies. And Joyce Flissler, also a Juilliard entry, would go over to enter the competition for violinists.

The conditioning of a contender for a great international musical meet is as strenuous, in its own way, as the conditioning of an Olympic athlete. Both require nothing less than the total human animal—physical, mental, emotional —filed down and fined down to hair-triggered fitness and timed for the instant of firing.

"We have only three months in which to get ready," Mme. Lhevinne told her candidate. "You must live as though you really were in training. See nobody and go nowhere five days of the week and be in bed by eleven."

Van worked six, eight, ten hours a day and still worried that he might not be ready by April. Mme. Lhevinne gave up her usual Sundays in the country to remain at home, so that she could hear him play. She was full of confidence, keenly aware that Van was bringing to the contest an absolute affinity for every part of the task. She had often been impressed with the natural flair and love he had for Russian music. In fact, later on somebody searched his family tree to see if there was not a Russian hidden somewhere in it, on the theory that the cause of his extreme responsiveness must

97

lie "in the blood." They found no one but the same old Anglo-Saxons and Celts as before.

Nonetheless, had he thought of it, he could have claimed kinship with Rachmaninoff by a sort of osmosis. When Josef Lhevinne was alive Rachmaninoff was a frequent visitor at his house. Rosina Lhevinne not only knew the composer's music from his own interpretations and comments, but, what was of immediate importance to Van right now, she knew how Russians liked to hear their music played. Van, of course, had been playing the Rachmaninoff Third with spectacular success all over God's country. But now he had to perform it on its native ground, from which sprouted indigenous ideas on interpretation. Yet according to Rosina Lhevinne, "Van's version of the Rachmaninoff Third got better and better. Not even Rachmaninoff ever played it better. It couldn't be done!"

Five days before Christmas, Mme. Lhevinne left for California to spend the holidays with her children. When she returned in mid-January she called Van—how was it coming? "Oh, thank goodness you're back!" he cried, almost leaping into the phone. "I must come right up and see you. Wait'll I tell you what happened to *me!*" In a short time he appeared at her door, so pale and emaciated that she was shocked at the sight. Shrugging out of his overcoat, he collapsed into a chair and blurted out the story. Remember those two communities he was booked to play in Ohio and Michigan? Well, he'd gone out there and had come down with the flu. He knew he had a fever but played the dates anyway. Flying back to New York, he had gone into a grocery to try to get some supplies and had fainted on the spot. He'd been in bed almost ever since. Two or three precious weeks completely lost——!

No, but wait; it wasn't all that bad. A friend had recommended this "wonderful doctor"—a man who had conditioned some of the athletes for the Olympic games. The doctor had already started to build him up with a new health regime—vitamins, shots, raw eggs, and six envelopes of Knox gelatin a day. He was beginning to feel better. And he wouldn't have to pay anything at all if he didn't win the competition. That's how sure the doctor was that he'd win.

Mme. Lhevinne was sufficiently intrigued to try the gelatin herself. She reported that it seemed to pick up her stamina. And in almost no time Van regained his old bounce and was back in the galleys. But now not only his health but also his confidence was flourishing.

What began to bother companionable Van, as March drew nearer, was the thought of that long, long, interminable flight over Atlantic nothingness, with no friend to talk to, no fellow spirit to share the experience. Always with Van the need to share experience is vital, fundamental.

"He wanted me to go with him, but of course I had to stay at Juilliard," says Rosina Lhevinne.

"He wanted me to go with him, and I would have loved to; but of course I couldn't leave," Sascha Greiner told me.

"He wanted me to go with him, but I told him to go alone," Mrs. Leventritt testifies. She also told him it would be the finest thing that ever happened to him if he went alone and won. Or even if he didn't win but went alone and stood on his own two feet. "Later on I know he was glad he listened."

Around the first of March, Gabriel Reiner of the Cosmos Travel Bureau, Inc., was approached by a tall, blond young customer who said he had been recommended to the agency by Mr. Schubart. He had to go to Moscow for the Tchai-

kovsky Competition but hadn't much money. He would like
to go tourist.

Oh yes, said Mr. Reiner, who negotiated contacts with
the U.S.S.R.; he had heard of the contest. Shostakovich had
written him a letter, asking how it might be given publicity
in the United States, and Ross Parmenter had been good
enough to publish a notice about it in *The New York Times*.
Mr. Reiner could book the young man on the SAS flight
912 of March 24, bound for Copenhagen. The name? How
do you spell Cliburn? It would be necessary, of course, to
await the arrival of a visa from the U.S.S.R.

The awaiting started. Van kept calling back impatiently
and dropping in to inquire. "Don't worry," said Mr. Reiner,
"I have often done business with the Soviets. It takes a little
time." Finally he volunteered: "Look. I know the president
of the Intourist Bureau; I'll call him in Moscow and see if
he can help." The president of Intourist, it developed, was
also a member of the committee for the Tchaikovsky Competition. The visa came through at the next-to-the-last moment: March 22. Van then switched passage to Air France
in order to go by way of Paris and connect with jet at Prague.

There was just time for a last-minute theater party to
honor Nola Rhodes' birthday. And a last-minute bon voyage
party at the Leventritts'—turkey for him, champagne for
the others—and the boy was off to Moscow, telephone bill
unpaid.

In one of his travel-worn suitcases were three hundred
vitamin capsules and pills, with directions from his doctor,
and a supply of Knox gelatin.

Forty hours later he was being driven in a car over the
stones of Red Square, craning his neck to catch the first

glimpse of onion-shaped domes against the pale sky. He was aware of just what to look for, a scene he knew by heart; for on the second Christmas after he and his parents had moved to Kilgore someone had given him a child's picture-book history of the world. Its bright illustrations had absorbed him to the exclusion of everything else. He pored over the photographs: the Parthenon of Greece, India's Taj Mahal, Westminster Bridge, the Tower of London, Versailles, the Washington Monument. But the picture that fascinated him most was the ancient Church of St. Basil in Moscow, with its seven curiously beautiful onion-shaped turrets, all of different colors, spiraling upward.

There it was now!—so unbelievably real and immediate, so like an old friend that tears of welcome sprang to the eyes. Then his glance moved along to massive gray walls, to great frowning façades, to the pomp and circumstance of battlements and parapets frozen in stone. For all the world like a Hollywood set——

So this was the Kremlin!

The U.S.S.R. was playing host to forty-eight young artists from nineteen different countries—China, Japan, France, Great Britain, the United States, Germany, Hungary, Poland, the far Russian provinces—and they were doing it up handsomely. Each "guest" of the government was housed at Moscow's new Hotel Peking in a suite of his own with a living room, bedroom, and bath, telephone, television, and short-wave radio. A special dining room was set aside for the use of contestants.

Cars were provided for sightseeing tours and trips to the opera, theater, or ballet; buses whisked them from the door of the hotel to the door of the conservatory. At all times an interpreter was at hand to bridge the gulf of language, and it seemed they had merely to breathe on this Russian genie's lamp, and the magic deed was done. To some of the aspirants from the freedom-loving West, unaccustomed to such pampering, it must have appeared, ironically enough, as though they had never had it so good. Materially, anyway. Or was that part of the conjuror's genius?

The first morning after Van arrived in Moscow his interpreter, Henrietta Balaieva, took him to the conservatory, where he met some of the sixteen judges and some of his fellow contestants. Then he was shown to his own practice studio, available to him day and night, whenever he wished to use it.

The same courtesies had been extended to the twenty-eight violin competitors, who had already finished their finals and had departed, the losers to their homes and homelands, the eight winners off for triumphant tours of the key Russian cities. First honors in the violin contest had been carried off by Valery Klimov, a Soviet artist. America's entrant, Joyce Flissler, had won seventh prize. She and her accompanist, Harriet Wingreen, also from Juilliard, had been immediately booked to appear in Leningrad, Kiev, Riga, and Odessa.

After they returned home they told me that everywhere they went in Russia, following the contest, they were stopped in the street by crowds, their pictures were snapped, they were asked for their autographs, they were feted and petted and hailed as "winners." To the Russians it was a wonderful accomplishment to have placed anywhere among the eight violinists chosen from the entire world, and so they honored all accordingly, with little discrimination for win, place, or show. What a contrast to the icy silence that awaited these two when they returned to New York! But more of that later.

Van had not been in Russia twenty-four hours, of course, before he found friends. "The first day when I went to the conservatory to practice I heard a knock at my door. A smiling young man entered and said in English, 'Welcome to Moscow—my name is Eduard Miansarov but call me Eddik.' We spent the next two hours playing and singing together."

Another pianist soon joined them and became the third member of the youthful musketeers: Naum Shtarkman, one of the Soviets' most esteemed young talents. "From then on, Eddik and Naum and I stuck together throughout our musical ordeal."

In Russia the order of places on the program is determined by drawing lots, or holding a sortition, as they call it. Van's turn in the preliminaries would be coming up on April 2, which gave him about a week in which to practice. He hurled himself into it. Yet in spite of his obsession with work and the beckonings of a new environment, he had the time and forethought to remember that Rosina Lhevinne was giving a concert for the Josef Lhevinne Scholarship Fund at Juilliard on March 28. She received a cablegram from Moscow: "MY LOVE AND THOUGHTS ARE WITH YOU. TREMENDOUS EXCITEMENT AND JOY." One of the first things he had looked for at the conservatory were the names of Josef Lhevinne and Rosina Bessie inscribed among the Gold Medal winners on the great marble tablet; and there they were, after a half century, in still-gleaming letters.

On the Tuesday evening of April 1, those who were to play in the next day's hearings were allotted time to go into the Bolshoi Salle, the great hall of the conservatory, and try out the piano: a Steinway, incidentally, despite the fact that one of the features of the Tchaikovsky Festival was a proud exhibit of pianos "made in the U.S.S.R."

"I can never forget that night," Van says. "The contestant before me was in there practicing one of the *"Études Tableaux"* of Rachmaninoff. She was doing it very beautifully. I was walking back and forth outside. Just imagine this hall with its grandeur and its spaciousness and the columns and the marble and the beautiful heavy rugs all going up and down the deep staircases—— It's so unbelievable! Yet the acoustics, when it's empty or when it's full, are marvelous. Particularly this night, it was terribly impressive.

"I remembered the very, very famous men whose music still seemed to echo from the walls—Rachmaninoff, Tchaikovsky, Scriabin, Glinka, Moussorgsky—the men who built Russian music and gave it its own definite flavor and sound. I sat down and listened to those sounds, feeling like a little boy again, awed by the fact that I was here in the place where Rachmaninoff had studied and Tchaikovsky had taught. It made me forget myself so completely that I got over all my fears and was no longer nervous."

This is how Van Cliburn saw himself on the eve of combat. He did not neglect to telephone his parents in Kilgore to notify them of the time he would be playing and to elicit their spiritual support. They, in turn, elicited the support of the local ministers, and "later I learned that the ministers had asked the whole town to pray for me. My parents did not pray for me to win, because winning in their minds isn't always the best thing. They prayed that God's will be done."

The Moscow competition was not only open to the public, but was *the* cultural event of the '58 season. Said an

American who was there: "The contest gripped Muscovites as the World Series captivates us. The audience was so alive, the air seemed to crackle with attention. It was alert to the smallest detail that concerned the participants or even the judges." The international jury was headed by Emil Gilels, the most celebrated of Soviet pianists, and included among its European members France's Marquis de Gontaut-Biron and Britain's Sir Arthur Bliss. One American had been invited to serve on the jury but had not accepted.

Van started, at that very first preliminary, with Bach's B-flat Prelude and Fugue from Book I of the *Well Tempered Clavier*, followed by the Mozart C major Sonata, K. 330. When the last chord had ceased echoing, all those in the audience took a deep breath and then began to bang their palms together in thunderous applause. Van stood up to take a bow at the piano, then reseated himself to wait for the uproar to subside. They would not permit it. Four times he had to stand up to acknowledge their quadrupled ovation before they would permit him to go back to the keyboard. And this was for Mozart, mind you—not for Russian music. Next he played four études: Chopin's "Winter Wind," Op. 25, No. 11; Scriabin's Op. 8 in D-sharp minor; Rachmaninoff's "*Étude-Tableau*" in E-flat minor, Op. 39, and Liszt's "*Mazeppa*." The final piece was one required of all contestants: Tchaikovsky's Theme and Variations, Op. 19—which, of course, they knew and loved.

And by then they knew and loved Van Kleeberrn, was it? Vanya! Vanyushka! When would he play again? The semifinals on Monday? To the box office for tickets. And by the weekend the weary office was telling all customers: "No tickets left. Kleeberrn is playing. Call again tomorrow."

Of the forty-eight who had entered the contest, twenty-one were left for the semifinals.

In this session, on April 7, Van opened with Sergius Taneiev's Prelude and Fugue, followed by another Tchaikovsky work that was required of all contestants: the first movement of the Sonata in G major. However, the piece that brought them again to their feet in a rapture of enthusiasm was not Russian music—it was Chopin—the F minor Fantasy, which completely bowled them over by the searching quality and iridescence of its execution. And while they were still rocking from its impact he let them have it once more with the full force of our good old friend, the Liszt Twelfth Rhapsody. After that, if Van had jumped up and demanded the crown jewels of Catherine the Second, Czarina of all the Russias, the audience would probably have stormed the Kremlin Museum and flung them at his feet. He finished with an American composition: the Fugue from the Piano Sonata, Op. 26, of Samuel Barber. The second trial was over.

And then there were nine. Nine for the finals: one from Red China, one from Japan, one from Tiflis in Georgia, one from Bulgaria, one from France, two from Russia, and two from the United States. Daniel Pollack was still in the race, breathing hotly on Van. These would all be winners, but in what order? That would be decided by the concerto performances, to be played the latter part of the week with the Moscow State Symphony under Kiril Kondrashin.

For the finals, the Russians required that each contestant play one of Tchaikovsky's three piano concertos. By now no reader should have the slightest difficulty in naming which of the three "Kleeberrn" elected to play.

On April 8, Mark Schubart had arrived in the U.S.S.R.,

having flown over to the Scandinavian countries for the International Exchange Program and then moving on to Moscow as an observer. He ran into Van that same day at a reception given by Richard Davis, counselor to the American legation. After noticing the reaction of the other guests to Van and after talking to musicians who had attended the preliminaries, Schubart realized that "Vanya" was rapidly becoming the rage of the town. He alerted Max Frankel of *The New York Times* that something of interest might be about to take place. Frankel attended the finals and consequently scooped the nation on the Van Cliburn story. Our embassy in Moscow had looked the other way when United States entrants arrived for the Tchaikovsky Festival, being "tired of coming in second or third against the Russians." But now Ambassador Llewellyn Thompson and his wife decided to attend Friday night's finals.

It was just as well they did, for "everybody who was anybody" in the capital was there. In a prominent box sat Elizabeth, Dowager Queen of the Belgians, and ranged in solid ranks were the upper echelons of Soviet officialdom with their well-dressed wives, all in a mood of greatest anticipation. For three nights there had been queues outside the conservatory office, where hopeful students waited for tickets; and as the hour of performance drew near the militia had to be called out to handle the crowds. Those who had good seats smiled upon each other as persons of consequence; many of those who did not have tickets played a good-natured game with the police, trying to sneak in unnoticed or just gate-crashing. They were speedily given what, in the land of the free, is called the bum's rush. Mark Schubart describes the throng as "so vibrant, it was terrifying really . . . but, of course, tremendously rewarding."

By the time the Moscow State Symphony began to tune its instruments, there were fifteen hundred jammed into the Bolshoi Salle, where the huge blown-up photograph of Tchaikovsky, in medallion form, gazed back from behind the piano. Flowers decked the stage. Even those who had standing-room-only considered themselves fortunate, and they filled the back of the auditorium and the copious balconies.

When Van made his entrance, before he played a note, there were roars of applause. Audiences in Europe don't whistle, of course—that is like booing—but they do stamp their feet. These people stamped their feet, clapped their hands, and called out "Vanya, Vanyushka" as though greeting a hero who was also a beloved friend. Then, as conductor Kondrashin rapped for order, they settled down happily to hear what the boy from Texas proposed to do with their Tchaikovsky First.

When it was over, the outburst was volcanic and prolonged. Bows for Kondrashin, bows for the orchestra, repeated bows for Van.

Second item on the program: Rondo by Dimitri Kabalevsky. This solo, *pièce imposée*, written especially for the Festival, was required of all competitors and had been sent out by mail as soon as the composer had finished it. Van had received his copy in New York in early February and memorized the score in two or three days. But it takes time to assimilate a new work. Only the night before, Van had dragged Mark Schubart into his studio at the conservatory at two in the morning to hear the Kabalevsky and had played it four times before they were mutually happy with the result. It was a rather tricky piece technically, and the composer has since withdrawn it for revisions. For the Rondo, Van won a standing ovation.

After intermission, the Rachmaninoff. Four years before when the identical pianist had played the identical work with Saul Caston and the Denver Symphony, Allen Young in the *Denver Post* of December 8, 1954, had written:

> Playing Rachmaninoff's Third Piano Concerto in D minor, this tall Texan first loped along with almost casual ease. Before long he was showing stunning technique as he cast runs up and down the scale, and suddenly there were the richest and cleanest of chords cascading about, and his musicianship became unmistakable.
>
> It's quite a thing when a young musician steps forward and in natural exuberance shows he can create as much swift volume as the mighty. Yet when the substance of a lengthy and difficult concerto is grasped in its entirety and everything falls into just proportions with a sense of growth and creation, then you shout "Hurrah!"

This audience shouted "Hurrah!" in Russian. They leaped to their feet and nearly broke the sound barrier with the sheer vibration of their yells and applause. Throughout the pandemonium could be heard a rhythmic beating of palms and shouting in unison: "First prize! First prize!" It came from the conservatory students and quickly spread to others. Although there were yet six finalists still to be heard, some of the jurors, quite forgetful of their impartiality, were seen to be joining in the wild acclaim. Alexander M. Goldenweiser, the white-haired patriarch of Russian pianists, made his way down the center aisle muttering to every-

one, "Genius! Genius!" Never, he stated later, had he heard
the concerto so well performed since Rachmaninoff played it.

Backstage, Emil Gilels, chairman of the jury, was em-
bracing Van openly. So was Kondrashin. Finally, the judges
were forced to permit a violation of contest rules and send
the artist onstage again for a second acknowledgment of the
howling triumph. The members of the orchestra themselves
stood up, exuberantly clapping. It never had happened
before in the whole ninety-two-year history of the Moscow Conservatory—an eight-and-a-half minute, timed-by-
wrist-watch, yelling, screaming, standing ovation.

For Van this moment was really the zenith.

8

Big Russian Bear Hug

On April 12 the readers of *The New York Times* found a
two-column cut of a blond young bow-tied musician on the
very front page. Over it was the caption: RUSSIANS
CHEER U.S. PIANIST, 23. It was the homeland's first
hint of what was happening deep in the heart of Moscow.
"But," warned correspondent Frankel, "it is far from certain that Mr. Cliburn will win first prize in the competition."
Six of the nine finalists were still to be heard from, "all first
rate." In any event, the verdict could not be known until
Monday. Mr. Frankel was human enough to enjoy his
scoop, but too humane to report that following Van's Friday
night appearance, and before the next finalist appeared, a
large part of the audience, having heard what they came to
hear—their darling Vanyushka—simply got up and walked
out.

All weekend rumors about the contest decision had been
flying around Moscow, though the last of the finals were
not to be played until Sunday evening. Around midnight

Van left the hall with the rest of his confreres. They filed out as usual past a billboard which announced a forthcoming solo recital to be given by the winner the following Friday night. Naturally, a gaping blank had stood in the center ever since it had been put up. But earlier that evening someone had reached up and in the reserved space had boldly printed the name: VAN CLIBURN.

The weary contestants drifted toward their dining room at the Hotel Peking for a snack and a glass of tea. Muscovites are night owls; they never go to bed. And their visitors happily embraced the local custom. There they all sat, munching and sipping and chatting, but mainly waiting, when Eddik Miansarov came hurrying in, beaming, "Van, you've won!" he cried, flinging his arms around his friend.

Van shook his head. "You can't know that, Eddik, not yet. Nothing's official till tomorrow noon."

A moment later, Naum Shtarkman rushed in, bursting with his tidings. "Vanya, you've won. There's no question about it. I just heard the news." He too was beaming.

Again Van shook his head. He was still arguing stubbornly, when in hustled a uniformed official from the conservatory. "Vanyushka," he said with a large, knowing grin, "you'd better go up to your room and put on your white tie and tails." Then he announced, "Everyone is going back to the conservatory now." At this, Van stopped arguing, smiled weakly, and stood up to walk slowly out of the room. Alone in his suite, he found two things to do—get dressed and get to talk to Mother and Daddy in Kilgore.

Half the audience from the finals was milling around when they got back to the hall. At sight of the winner, flanked by his colleagues, the mob pressed forward and applauded. Motion picture cameras were all set up on the stage. The orchestra was tuning up once again, and Kondrashin was already on the podium. The prize-winning program was about to be recorded on color film for the millions of Russians who could not see or hear it "live." Van took his place at the keyboard—for a session that lasted until 5 A.M.

While this was going on Mark Schubart's telephone woke him back at the hotel. "Van's won!" Frankel crowed at him over the wire. Instantly wide-awake, Schubart sent off a cable to president Schuman at Juilliard: "WE ARE IN ORBIT."

The New York Times, for the second time in three days, slapped the bow-tied pianist across its Monday front page, and by this time Cliburn's victory dwarfed all other news on the nation's presses. To most readers it was the world's greatest story. Every bus driver and his passengers, every doorman and all his tenants . . . in fact, the world and his neighbor were buzzing with nothing else.

To others it carried more intimate meanings.

Allen and Hazel Spicer on Claremont Avenue stared at the headlines. "That's great," they said to one another. "At last he can afford that piano he bought for the church."

Gil Gallagher down at the Asti shook his head in perplexity. "It gets me," he observed, "why anyone with so much talent was forced to go all the way to Moscow to get across the street."

The waiters at the Carnegie Hall Tavern recognized their customer at once. "So he made it," one of them said. "Well, now he can order the full pot-roast dinner."

The Schuyler Chapins' ten-year-old son Henry, who studies 'cello, went to the door that morning to pick up the paper. "Look, Mommy, look!" he yelled, bounding back into the house. "My accompanist! My accompanist!"

It was some time later that Monday when Mme. Lhevinne and Bill Schuman got a phone connection through to Moscow. Both smile ruefully today when they relate the gist of that first conversation with Van. He must rest, they told him firmly, when he got back from Russia. "You've been pressing very hard. Now you'll need quiet, at least for the summer, and time to work on your repertoire." At that moment Van was as naïve as they and readily agreed.

Back in Moscow the Acceptance Ceremony was scheduled for the same evening. A few winks of sleep, then to the Kremlin at five in the afternoon to attend the reception of the Dowager Queen Elizabeth of Belgium. Her Majesty, founder of the international music competition in Brussels, indefatigable sponsor and lover of music, now in her eighties, had become one of Van's warmest admirers.

Her reception was attended by the Soviets' topmost brass: Marshal Voroshilov, chief of state; First Deputy Premier Mikoyan; and most notably, Premier Khrushchev, who had been out of town and had only just returned. While Van was having his audience with the Queen and Voroshilov he was approached with an unusual invitation. Although there was, of course, to be another Kremlin reception the next afternoon for the contest winners, would he, as a most highly esteemed guest, now care to be presented to Mr. Khrushchev?

"So I was taken to him," says Van, "and he was very cordial and gracious." As a matter of fact, he was much more than that. The pudgy leader of the Soviet Union threw his arms around Van, hugged him tightly, and bussed him on both cheeks. Then, cocking a merry eye up at his six-foot-four, Khrushchev asked through the interpreter:

"Why are you so tall?"

"Because I am from Texas," Van answered, never missing a plug for the old home state.

"You must have lots of yeast in Texas," Khrushchev countered.

"No—just vitamin pills."

Van has since kicked himself many times for missing a punch line. He wishes he'd said, "Yes, we do, and I come from 'Yeast Texas.'"

"How old are you?"

"I am twenty-three."

"My son is also twenty-three."

"What month was he born?" asked Van, who can dribble the ball of conversation along with any diplomat.

"I must ask his mother about that."

"Was it July?" Van's own birth month.

"Probably July." Why not?

This is the conversation that was so widely reprinted by papers at the time. What did not get much coverage was the fact that Khrushchev also went on to talk knowledgeably about Van's performances.

"I have heard so much about your wonderful interpretation and wonderful playing of the Chopin F minor Fantasy," he told Van. "I love that work, and I am disappointed I didn't get to hear it in the second preliminary. But I am looking forward very much to hearing you tonight."

"I shall never forget that he knew about the Chopin Fantasy," Van told me later in New York. "I will always appreciate it."

After the reception everyone moved on to the Acceptance Ceremony at the conservatory, where the three top winners, in both the piano and violin competitions, were scheduled to perform. As head of the jury, Emil Gilels announced the list of winners for piano:

1. Van Cliburn, U.S.A.
2. A tie: Liu Shih-kung, China; Lev Vlasenko, Tiflis, Georgia.
3. Naum Shtarkman, U.S.S.R.
4. Eduard Miansarov, U.S.S.R.
5. Milena Mollova, Bulgaria.
6. Nadia Gedda-nova, France.
7. Toioaki Matsuura, Japan.
8. Daniel Pollack, U.S.A.

Later, when Gilels was asked whether it had been difficult for the judges to decide on a first prize winner among so many gifted players, he revealed that the Cliburn choice had been immediate and unanimous.

Shostakovich, as chairman of the arrangement committee, presented Van and Valery Klimov, the winning violinist, with their engraved certificates, prize money, and shining Tchaikovsky Gold Medals. Van acknowledged his with a few words in Russian, memorized for the occasion, and evoked a round of applause. Then, as required, he and Kondrashin once more played the first movement of the Tchaikovsky Concerto. Pandemonium again broke loose when he finished, and there were insistent cries in English of "More! More!" He was forced to respond with three solo encores. Still there were cries of "More!" But Van, who had been performing for two days and nights with a bandaged finger, the result of a blister from constant playing, decided to call it a night. He raised his hands for attention and said in Russian, "Many thanks."

To grasp the full import of Van's triumph, it should be

known that the Russians always hold pre-competitions to select their representatives. From two hundred applicants the
top ten were weeded out and entered. Van had therefore
come up against the best Russia had to offer.

The ceremony concluded, the Bolshoi Salle was emptied
of people. But one hour later Van was back onstage with
Kondrashin and the orchestra for another filming session
which went on till 3:30.

Van at least had his victory to buck up his energies. But
he kept expressing concern for the members of the Moscow
State Symphony, who had been rehearsing three hours each
morning throughout the contest and performing as much
as four and a half hours each and every evening.

Back again to the hotel for a few more winks of sleep. And
forth again to the Great Kremlin Palace in the afternoon
for the Ministry of Culture's reception for the winners. This
time Khrushchev bore down on Van with hands outstretched, proudly presenting his son, daughter, and grand-
daughter. When the champagne was produced for a toast
Van shifted uneasily, tried to avoid the glass, then accepted
it smilingly and touched it to his lips. Do or die for Texas!
He pulled his one and only boner when he was introduced
to Nikolai Bulganin and addressed him as "Mr. Molotov."
No one seemed to mind.

In the midst of festivities Mikoyan said to Van, "You've
been a very good politician for your country. You've done
better than all the politicians." Khrushchev, who had assumed formal leadership of the Soviet government only
eighteen days before, nodded vehemently. "Here we are
without a round table," he pointed out, including the winner
from China and the other countries in his gesture, "having
an ideal example of peaceful coexistence." At this point,

someone suggested that the musicians might run things better without governments at all, and the Premier agreed good-naturedly.

By now everyone who even looked like an American was being stopped in the streets of Moscow and congratulated on "your victory." A United States diplomat was told, "Now you *really* have a sputnik!" Moscow Radio was proclaiming "the American sputnik—developed in secret." The big names of Soviet music filled up columns in the newspapers with professional estimates of the American's playing and musicianship.

"Genius!" declared pianist Sviatoslav Richter, one of Russia's greats and a member of the jury. ". . . a word I do not use lightly about performers."

Stated composer Aram Khachaturian: "You find a virtuoso like this only once or twice in a century."

Shostakovich, in *Pravda*, pronounced him a "phenomenally skilled musician with brilliant, unduplicated individuality." And the dean of Soviet composers clung to the misapprehension that Van had previously remained totally unknown in the land of his birth.

Whenever Van stepped out of doors he was trailed around by adoring crowds. Every once in a while when solicitous friends thought he was about to fall apart they would lock him in his room to protect him from worshipers. But that did not always work. One appeared from nowhere, in the middle of his room, in the middle of the night. Russian bobby-soxers swarmed about the exits of the conservatory, waiting for him to finish his long hours of practice. When female admirers heard he was losing weight (twelve pounds, in spite of all his vitamins) they brought him bags of oranges. Total strangers, men and women both, stopped him in the street to hug and kiss him. Mme. Khrushchev sent a bouquet.

The fantastic, incredible week did not end until the bone-tired and happy hero gave that solo recital on Friday and appeared at two more performances with other winners. To the delight of music students and teen-agers who arrived early, Van warmed up with warbled renditions of "Blue Moon" and "Embraceable You."

No matter what he did, his public was with him every note of the way. Once, Van cut loose in the midst of a stormy passage and broke a piano string. His hearers were full of sympathy for him and took it, of course, merely as additional proof of Vanya's terrific emotional intensity. "The Russians love their virtuosos the way the Italians love their opera singers," wrote Mark Schubart to *The New York Times*. "And when the big pieces of the Russian literature were being played, every flubbed passage was greeted with audible sighs of dismay, always regretful, never contemptuous."

When Moscow TV announced it would televise half of the prize-winning performance indignant protests flooded the station. Half? They wanted *all*, which they got "by popular demand," right to the last note of the last encore.

Over in the next hemisphere Mme. Lhevinne was summoned to her telephone. "How would you like to hear Van?" a friend inquired. "Hold the receiver——" As the volume on a short-wave set was turned up Madame heard the familiar tones of Van's way with the Rachmaninoff Third, followed by the voice of a Russian woman announcer. Madame, it seems, was proving of some solace to Soviet pride. To be sure, the announcer said, an American had won first prize, but had he not been taught by a Russian?

Nevertheless, Americans would have been pleased to know that just as we at home had been criticizing our methods of education as compared to the Russian methods ("What Is Wrong with Our Teaching of Science?"), so the Russians now began to write and lecture on "What Is Wrong with Our Teaching of Music?"

For quite a time, the United States had smugly taken it for granted that she was foremost in scientific and technological development, while the U.S.S.R. had complacently assumed that her People's Artists were the world's finest. For two years she had been "feeding out" some of her more prodigious artists—pianist Gilels and violinist Oistrakh—to permit the outside world to bear witness to their formidable interpretative prowess. And mighty artists they are. But somehow the impression had been created abroad that, in someone's phrase, "Behind that Curtain, they had nothing but golden monsters with twenty-four fingers."

When pianist Richter recently asserted, without exaggeration, "Everybody used to be afraid of us Russians," he was referring to a time some years since when a French music official advised a Russian performer that the committee would prefer Soviet competitors not to enter: they frightened off contestants from other lands. All this had been changed now, and some agonizing reappraisal was going on.

"The mass shortcoming of our musicians is their leveling," suggested critic Vartanyan of the *Sovetskaya Kultura*. "Many lack bright lines of character. One of the main reasons lies in that chief attention in training Soviet pianists was given to the development of the technical side, and *the problem of development of creative individuality* remained out of the field of vision." The italics are mine, for the statement is extremely revealing as a sample of recent Soviet self-examination. Also noteworthy is the fact that Van, whose accomplishments caused this soul-searching, was thereby held in even greater esteem and affection.

He further endeared himself when he "made the pilgrimage" to Tchaikovsky's home at Klin, now a museum and national shrine. He stood in awe before the Master's treasured piano. Only the greatest pianists are permitted to play it and then only on Tchaikovsky's birthday. But the birthday would not be till May 7, and this was April. By tacit consent Tchaikovsky's birthday was "moved up" a few weeks to make it official, and Vanyushka played.

He met and talked with the composer's great-great nephew. From the grave he dug a handful of earth, the first part of a projected errand of sentiment. A group had called upon Van one day, tenderly bearing a half-grown shrub. They'd heard, they told him, that he wanted a white Russian lilac to take home and plant on Rachmaninoff's grave. They had all stood in long lines for tickets to his concerts but had been unable to get in. So they had pooled their money and bought him the lilac. Would he accept it, kindly, with their gratitude?

Van bore the shrub into his hotel suite and watered it daily—not quite with tears, but with a feeling that was very near to reverence. Who would not respond to the simple outpouring of loving hearts? Little wonder that the Russians' favored guest sometimes, in the heat of his exuberant response to such freely given warmth and affection, reciprocated with some perfectly well-meant but ill-advised protestations which, when reported in the American press, did not make for enthusiastic reading back home.

In each of the cities where Van played after Moscow

—Leningrad, Riga, Kiev, Minsk—his performances were
broadcast over TV and radio. Notwithstanding, he learned
upon his arrival in Leningrad that the conservatory students had mobbed the box office when they were unable to
get tickets. Van insisted on admitting them to the afternoon
rehearsal and on playing the entire program. The response
was overwhelming; so much so that he was to make it a
regular feature of his concerts back in the states. But not
only students struggled for admission. For three days and
three nights an unbroken line had circled the hall, and in
the midst of Van's evening performance one woman fell to
the floor in an exhausted faint.

In every city there was such a gold-rush demand for his
recordings that the factory couldn't press them fast enough.
Sue Bachner Rothman, a friend of ours who arrived in Russia two weeks after Van left, wrote to Constance and me:

> GUM, the largest department store in Moscow, per-
> haps in Russia, has a record section in an annex across
> the street. There, in the classical division, is a tray full
> of post cards. You fill one out with your name and ad-
> dress, and the name of the recording you want. You pay
> for the postage, and when the recording becomes avail-
> able, the card is mailed to you. Then you come in and
> buy your record.
>
> The stack of cards filed behind Van Cliburn's name
> is enormous; those behind other names, even those of
> Gilels and Oistrakh, minute by comparison. We were
> told that *never* had there been so many requests as they
> had for Cliburn's two concertos. While I was waiting,
> an American correspondent's wife, a Russian general, a
> young Mongol couple, our guide, and a dozen teen-

agers added their names to the list. Most, incidentally, ordered both recordings.

P.S. Cliburn's attraction for the girls is tremendous. "Is he married?" they ask. Besides his magnificent playing, they admire his luxuriant head of hair. Bushy or curly hair is now definitely *à la mode!* . . . for men and women. By the way, chalk up one for the distaff side: we heard of many families who had a terrible problem deciding which member would use the one ticket they could get for Van's concerts, and we gathered that the wives usually won out.

And everywhere he went there were people coming toward him, smiling and holding out presents. Such presents!

From the faculty and students of Leningrad State Conservatory, a landscape painted by one of their professors.

From a Russian family, a huge porcelain plate with a troika painted upon it, treasured in their family for seventy years. "Look at it in your bad moments," read the note that came with it, "and think there are people who love you and always will."

From the daughter of Vassily Safonov, once director of the Moscow Conservatory and Josef Lhevinne's teacher, a priceless photograph of Safonov taken with Tchaikovsky nearly three quarters of a century before.

From Minister of Culture Vladimiroff, a huge Pinocchio-like doll with a humorous card pointing out that the doll and and the donor were equally bald.

From Moscow admirers, a prized leather-bound volume of Shakespeare's sonnets.

From the Central Museum of Music Culture, a biography of Rachmaninoff.

From a student in Minsk, an etching of his hero, Van-yushka, done from a photograph. "Forgive us if sketch is imperfect," said the inscription in English. "It was drawn not by artist, but by future pianist."

From students of the State Conservatory of Latvia, a recording of the Shostakovich First Symphony made by the Bolshoi Theater Orchestra and autographed by Kondrashin.

From the Director of the Theater Academy in Moscow, a Russian balalaika.

From Henrietta Balaieva, his interpreter, a recording of Rachmaninoff's *Aleko*.

From an admirer, a medallion of Tchaikovsky with a card inscribed, "To the Raphael of the Piano—Van Cliburn, Moscow, 1958."

Nor did they forget Mamushka Kleeberrn, of whom they had read. To her they sent a gold and white satin evening bag with matching white kid gloves, amber and silver jewelry, beautifully packaged bottles of perfume, samples of modern Russian ceramics and antique Russian enamels, cigarette boxes fashioned of malachite.

And in addition to all this——

Music scores, albums, woodcuts, silver spoons, tea sets, samovars. Many of the presents had obviously been stored away at the bottom of some chest or trunk through long years, through revolutions and wars, and finally brought out, refurbished, and presented to one at last deserving of so cherished a tribute.

Probably no living American has met so many Russians—hugged them, kissed them, shaken hands with them, slapped and been slapped by them, jabbered at them incomprehensibly through smiling interpreters. Yet pressure was so great that he did not see too much of Russia itself. In the early days before the finals he had sometimes slipped away from the cars and buses at his constant disposal to ride the fabulous subway. Child of the BMT and Independent, how could he believe in a rapid-transit system that had statues and pictures instead of chewing-gum ads? Nor could he get over the wonder of the electronic buttons that showed you the way—press the proper key and a map of the route lighted up.

For the rest: a few stolen hours blissfully roaming the galleries of the Hermitage Museum in Leningrad; a visit to the Bolshoi Theater to see Khachaturian's spectacular new ballet, *Spartak*; to the opera for Rachmaninoff's *Francesca da Rimini* and *Aleko*, never performed in any other part of the world; to the studio of Bachic-Serbien to have a life mask made for the conservatory collection; and to Kondrashin's home to see the new baby. All else was just work.

Van's last out-of-town concert was played at Minsk on May 9. That night he boarded the train for Moscow at two in the morning. "I took an excellent Russian sleeping pill and slept until noon. I felt ready to go."

He was met at the station by some members of the American Embassy. "We hadn't been able to get together since I'd been in Moscow, so I said, 'Today is my American Embassy day.' We spent the whole time together.

"At two o'clock Sunday morning I crawled into bed and tried to get a little sleep, because at eleven Sunday night I was to begin a long recording session. Leonard Warren, of the Met, was singing at the Bolshoi that evening, and I went backstage to say hello. After Warren had left and the stage had been cleared, the orchestra came on, the piano was tuned, and we started to record. That session lasted till half past five Monday morning.

"Then, of course, whenever you do something that draws on the nervous system you don't want to sleep afterward. You just want to eat. So we all ate, and talked, and I went to bed for maybe two hours. Later in the day we did a film at the Children's School, and I was supposed to do a four-hour recording session for solo repertoire that night. But I just had to cancel."

That same Monday he learned that Columbia Artists Management had finalized arrangements for his first concert on May 19 at Carnegie Hall. And they wanted Kondrashin to conduct for him. Van also wanted Kondrashin. Kondrashin dearly wanted to come. But would it be possible?

"Now we had to concentrate on getting Kiril's visa. I made four or five calls to the U.S.A., but no one could tell me anything definite. Finally, we got a very hurried call from Mr. Mikoyan's office saying that everything was cleared and Kiril could go. Wonderful! I called New York at once to tell them yes, they could have Kondrashin.

"At last I got to bed at around one o'clock. Tuesday afternoon we had recording sessions of the Tchaikovsky Concerto at the Bolshoi which lasted from three till seven-thirty in the evening. After that I simply had to see Rachmaninoff's *Francesca*."

Time was growing short now. "I had to say my farewells but was told the orchestra wanted me to hear a retake on the *prestissimo* section of the Tchaikovsky. I listened and said I thought we should do it over again. But Kiril said, 'No, it's fine. And anyway, the orchestra wants to say good-by to you.'

"The orchestra members were all sitting around. I was feeling very sad, for we had been onstage together for a total of forty-five hours since I came to Moscow.

" 'We have something for you,' they said, and the personnel manager came forward and presented me with a beautiful album containing a complete picture-history of my stay in Russia, with photographs of all the places I had been. And on top of that, they gave me a box of exquisite Russian art-work enamel illustrating scenes from Pushkin's fairy tales. It was filled with wonderful Russian chocolates. There was an enamel cigarette case, and also a poster of our last concert together, autographed by every member of the orchestra."

That final concert, on the day before he was to leave, was televised to seventeen million people.

The inexorable bans of monetary law permitted him to take only half his prize money beyond the frontiers of Russia. "If the Ministry of Culture will approve the plan," he proposed, "I'd like to give part of my winnings to establish two memorial prizes at the Moscow Conservatory in the name of two great pianists—Josef Lhevinne and Rachmaninoff, who both graduated from the Moscow Conservatory the same year and received gold medals."

He added: "I'd like to see three prize-winning Russian pianists—Lev Vlasenko, Naum Shtarkman, and Eduard Miansarov—go to the United States to perform for Americans."

On the morning of May 14, television cameras were trained on the airfield at Moscow to record for the Russian people the very last moments of Van Kleeberrn on Soviet soil. A huge crowd closed ranks to hear the short speech of farewell which he had memorized in Russian. Henrietta was glowing with pride that he was doing it so well. Eddik and Naum, all his friends, the dignitaries of the conservatory, students and admirers stood waving and waving as the big SAS plane took to the air and veered off for Copenhagen. Van, pressing his tear-stained face against the window, watched the figures below grow smaller and smaller. . . .

He leaned back a long time before he looked at the post card which had been thrust into his hand at the very last minute. On its front was a picture of the familiar conservatory, with its columned façade. He turned it over. Filling the whole back of the card, a closely written message in English:

Dear Van:

It is just a quick card from some of your admirers to tell you how enormously gratefull we all are to you for those moments of unforgettable emotional uplift that you so lavishly bestowed on us. We shall always think back with a kind of nostalgia mingled with deep satisfaction on the wonderful days of April and May of 1958. It was a *marvellous* experience and we, students of Moscow Conservatoire, feel so fortunate to have gone through it.

Now that you are leaving we would feel utterly disconsolate were it not for our hope to see and hear you back in Moscow someday *in not too distant future*. And this is really something for us to live by. We pray that you may always serve the noblest art of all—music —as sincerely and devotedly as you do now. And that your God-given talent may flourish unceasingly. Blessings and God speed you. Yours affectionately,

Fellow Musicians

"Blessings and God speed you." It was not the first time Van had been struck by the prevalence of such phrases in the common speech of Russia.

He had promised to return . . . in perhaps a year's time. Who knows? But Kiril would be following him the very next day across the sky.

9

88 Keys to the City

The New York taxi driver stepped on his brakes as he saw the detour signs. "What's goin' on here?" he yelled to the cop . . . "A parade? Fer the *piano player?*"

His incredulity was entirely reasonable, even in the face of the actuality—the biggest city on earth greeting a musician with the honors usually reserved for gold-braided generals, visiting heads of state, Channel swimmers, and other national heroes. From the Battery to City Hall the sidewalks were lined with popeyed, waving, ecstatic noonday crowds shrieking out a welcome to the towheaded Texan who had "showed them Russians," while from the canyon walls looming above him the ticker tape came swirling down in tangled spools of snow.

Was all this because Van Cliburn was the first American musician to win a contest abroad? Hardly. Within six previous years Leon Fleisher had won the Queen of Belgium Piano Prize, at least as demanding a contest as the one at Moscow; John Browning came "within a sixteenth note" of capturing first place in the same Brussels competition four years later, losing by only half a vote to Russia's Ashkenazy; and Berl Senofsky took first prize at the Violin Competition. Leslie Parnas walked off with first prize at the First International Casals Competition for 'cellists in Paris; violinist Sidney Harth won second prize in a photo finish (missing first by merely three points out of nine hundred) at the Wieniawski International Competition in Poznan, Poland. And in exactly the same month that Van Cliburn won in Moscow, Ivan Davis, also of Texas, won first prize in piano at Naples.

That is part of the record, even without mentioning such previous artistic victories on home soil as Seymour Lipkin's capture of the Rachmaninoff Award and Gary Graffman's capture of its special prize, in a competition that represented the most searching and stringent test ever held in our country.

But how many knew and how many cared? How many who sell and buy musical services, how many music lovers were responsive to these accolades? Primarily, a few alert members of the musical press, notably Howard Taubman of *The New York Times*. The gist of Taubman's argument was contained in the head and subhead of one of his most forceful Sunday articles:

WHAT PROFITS IT

For an American to Win a Major Prize In Europe?——Not Much at Home

Is it any wonder that Van was as dazed as the rest of us or that he kept saying that day, over and over, "It's a dream! And if it is, I hope I never wake up." There were many who

saw his life as a vertiginous nightmare rather than a dream,
but Van savored every aspect of its unreality.

The New York celebration was initiated when a hastily
appointed committee met one afternoon at the Department
of Commerce and Public Events. Commissioner Richard
C. Patterson, Jr., Assistant Commissioner Emma Rothblatt,
and John Effrat of the Actor's Fund of America outlined
the Mayor's original desire to stage a worthy welcome for
the conquering hero on his return. Plans were then formu-
lated for a colossal Van Cliburn Day Parade on May 20, to
be followed by a luncheon at the Waldorf, to which Mayor
Wagner would invite some five hundred guests.

Schools and colleges were asked to declare holidays. The
music schools were asked to get out and march, with pen-
nants flying and bands playing. Soon the idea developed
into the concept of an American Music Day, to honor not
only Cliburn but also "all New York City music students,
music teachers, and music lovers." It was assumed that
everyone even remotely associated with music would rally
round joyously.

Musicians, however, can gripe along with the best of 'em
—longshoremen, steel workers, or plasterers. A sizable group
of artists and educators viewed with deep suspicion this
abrupt attempt to woo their allegiance, and they raised quiz-
zical eyebrows at Father Knickerbocker's sudden admission
that musicians existed at all. Six days before the parade the
New York Herald Tribune let a whole bag of felines loose
upon the town with the three-column story: PARADE FOR
PIANIST LAGS.

A number of the city's leading music schools and university music departments, it seems, hadn't even bothered
to answer Commissioner Patterson's telegrams. Others had

begged off, explaining that examination time was approaching and that, in any case, their music departments were not set up for marching or for supplying bands, as requested. The First Army declined to furnish its usual ticker-tape band because someone had decided the event was "too commercial"—and was promptly put in its place by being told that nobody wanted a military representation, anyway.

Some of the other reasons offered for refusing the city's invitation: The city is trying to capitalize on the Russian ovation to Cliburn; it's a political gesture. Top winners of this country had never been so honored before; why the change of heart? Only private philanthropy assists American prize winners to go abroad to win such honors; why should public authorities, which have given no help, jump on the band wagon? And finally, a group of mixed explanations, evidencing "plain pique"; some would simply not march in Caesar's triumph.

Yet in spite of this resistance Van Cliburn's welcome was probably the most explosive, emotionally, of any staged since the day of the Lindbergh triumph. Stenographers, receptionists, office boys, and executives shouted and cheered, leaning far out over sills to watch the long, gangling figure that half sprawled, half perched atop the open Imperial that inched up lower Broadway.

Only two cars were in the motorcade, one for Van and one for the officials. Escorting them were troupes of marching youngsters, bands, choruses, majorettes, cheerleaders, baton twirlers, fife-and-drum corps, and all the pageantry and mummery that go into the making of a gala parade. Teen-agers with hands outstretched ran up to the car. One very pretty, starry-eyed girl raised up on tiptoe and demanded

a kiss. Van nearly fell out of the car fulfilling the order—
smack on the lips.

And there were the cool cats, too. "Give us five, Van,"
said one high school student, jogging alongside and reaching
up a hand. Van gave him five with the old iron grip. Men
on the route of progress eyed with suspicion the bristling
bush of hair, wilder than ever from the ministrations of Moscow barbers. Some voiced their opinions with a freeman's
candor: "Where's your fiddle?" Van only waved back, laughing. And anyway, as one spectator put it: "So he needs a
haircut? So what? So did Paderooski!"

While planning the parade someone on the committee
had begun to worry about the weather that day. What if
it rains? Bill Judd, who by now had seen his boy come zoom-
ing through two competitions he had advised him not to
enter, was finally convinced of the Cliburn luck. "Don't
worry," he said, with an oracular smile. "On Van Cliburn
Day the weather will be *perfect*." And it was.

Meantime, those attending the Mayor's luncheon at the
Waldorf-Astoria had been seated at their tables, patiently
waiting since 12:30. "Some guests, hungrier than others, began to dig into their halibut flakes Antoine," noted *The New
Yorker's* Man-about-Town. "Harry Hirshfield glanced impatiently at his watch. Someone must have gummed up the
ticker-tape parade for Van Cliburn and the subsequent
ceremonies at City Hall——"

Nobody had gummed up anything at all. It was just that
the presentations and acceptances of the city's Scroll for Exceptional and Distinguished Services and the Medallion of
the City of New York, with the attendant speeches, take
more time than anyone can estimate. An invocation was
spoken by the Reverend Richard R. Hamilton of Calvary

Baptist Church; the Mayor read his Proclamation; Commissioner Patterson extended greetings on behalf of the town; Robert Dowling of ANTA made an address; and Van responded to all.

The hands on my wrist watch stood at one-twenty when Van finally strode into the Empire Room, His Honor the Mayor jogging alongside. As they made their way to the dais the national anthem broke out and everyone jumped to attention. The second the music stopped, dozens of people swarmed from their tables and rushed toward Van to hug and be hugged, to have autographs signed, or just to take a look.

While the rest of us were tackling our entree the guest of honor hardly swallowed a mouthful. He had just learned that Robert Dowling was leaving that afternoon for Moscow. Van composed a letter to his Russian friends. Not just a scrawl, but a beautifully organized, long message, which he read aloud to the gathering before handing it to Dowling.

Mother Cliburn looked regal. Father Cliburn sat beside her, gazing about him with unconcealed disbelief. The important officials and citizens of the City of New York were in that room paying homage to the youngster whose future he had tried to protect with insurance; and now, from what people were saying, the boy was likely to make more money this year than General Motors!

Bill Schuman got up to speak for Juilliard—"Your alma mater is proud of you, Van." Richard Rodgers raised a toast to "this young, this very old diplomat." And Rosina Lhevinne was presented with an inscribed vase from the city, the first Van Cliburn Award, "to be presented annually." All of us made speeches.

But there was one young woman who neither made a speech nor was called upon to take a bow. She was Joyce Flissler, the violinist who had gone through the same fire and brimstone of the Moscow competition but who had come out in seventh place. She sat there watching hundreds of people going mad over Van. Liking him personally, she was happy at his fortune. But how could she help feeling a slow sadness in observing her anonymity in her own country, and on this particular occasion, as compared to the genuine appreciation she had received in Russia?

Although it had been stipulated, at the very first meeting of the planning committee, that "other winners of the Tchaikovsky Festival" should take part in the honors, the thought had been lost somewhere along the way. Daniel Pollack, who had toured and recorded extensively in Russia, remained abroad. But New York-born Joyce Flissler had returned home and was completely available to participate in the festivities. Nevertheless, her being there at all was almost accidental. A city official had called her management, the National Music League, to ask for suggestions in regard to the guest list. "Well, for goodness' sake," said N.M.L., "first and foremost Joyce Flissler, who was also a winner!"

"Oh, fine. How do you spell her name? Where does she live?"

That is how she got there. She walked in, knew only a few people, was known to no others, and sat down with a friend who was also alone. Not one speaker was alerted to her presence. I discovered it only a week later by happenstance, when a visitor to my office asked whether I had known that Miss Flissler was at the luncheon. I was astounded. Without bothering to answer I got her on the phone immediately in an attempt to apologize and explain.

Miss Flissler said, "Oh, that's all right. I admire Van, and he certainly deserved the reception. As for me, there hasn't been any sign of recognition since I returned, and this was just one more little pill along with the others." Then she went on to tell me that in Russia she was offered the identical tour that Van played. She couldn't accept it, since she is married to a member of the New York Philharmonic, just then due to leave on its South American tour, and she had to return home to take care of her children.

David Oistrakh, who had been warm in praise of her work, had deplored the fact that she could not remain in Russia for all the engagements offered her. "My dear," he said, "I assure you that you can always have a fine career among us whenever you come back. Make it soon."

"That in itself was worth everything," she told me. "Hearing his opinion, delighting in his graciousness, and being asked to return."

The brusque awakening came from her management after she got home. Not one American engagement, not one inquiry resulted from her accomplishment. There was no more interest in her now than in the pre-Moscow Flissler. Her management kept sending press releases on her Russian reception: practically nothing got in.

We Americans do not relish hearing any phase of our culture unfavorably compared to that of the Russians. It is time, however, that once and for all we scrap our "winner-take-all" philosophy.

Van had landed at Idlewild Airport four days before the parade. Arriving with him were seventeen pieces of luggage —in contrast to the three he had departed with—and one white lilac bush that would have to remain in quarantine till cleared by the authorities. On hand to greet him were his parents, accompanied by a posse of friends who had come all the way up from Texas to welcome him. To the battery of reporters who asked the inevitable question, "What do you think of your success?" he replied with a smile, "I'm not a success. I'm only a sensation." And to those who wondered how he had hit it off so well with the Russians he gave the reassuring answer: "It must be because there's just a bit of Texas in the Russians. And I *told* them so!"

"Weren't you afraid you might lose to a Communist pianist?" he was asked.

"I wonder if the Communist pianists were afraid they might lose to a Republican or Democratic or Gaullist pianist?" he shrugged.

Formalities over, he was whisked by limousine to the Hotel Pierre on Fifth Avenue, where he was startled to find he had a suite with not one but two living rooms. An adjacent suite was occupied by his parents. The moment he saw the Steinway parlor grand in the second living room he lunged forward and swept his hands up and down the keys in happy anticipation. However, the luggage came up. Suitcases were snatched open to display souvenirs and presents, and the piano in no time became as deeply piled with impedimenta as the rest of the ménage. A portent of things to come.

I first encountered the post-Moscow Van the day after his arrival. That Saturday afternoon Constance and I had seen the Utrillo exhibition at the Hammer Galleries. The day was brilliant and beautiful, and as we walked up Fifth Avenue and passed the Pierre, Constance had the sudden thought: "Let's just pop in and leave a greeting for Van at the desk." In the lobby we ran into Bill Judd. "Wouldn't you like to *see* Van?" he asked, with the subdued manner of one who inquires, "Would you care to view the remains?"

In silence we all rode up to the twenty-second floor. Arriving at the suite, Judd produced a key from his pocket and furtively unlocked the door. He preceded us into a large foyer, beyond which was a huge, stately living room with the drapes and blinds half drawn. Solemnly seated in the semidarkness around a table set for luncheon was an all-stag group: Alan Kayes of RCA Victor; concert manager Frederick Christopher Schang III, the best Russian linguist of the crowd; conductor Harry John Brown; Papa Cliburn; Van himself, and Kiril Kondrashin, whom Van had met at Idlewild that morning.

All had been talking in low, hushed tones. As we entered they stopped their murmuring and stood, slowly and simultaneously, as though someone had just intoned, "And now, let us rise." The sober scene was in astonishing contrast to the swirl of merriment we had anticipated on greeting our victorious Van. As we hugged each other without saying a word, my memory plunged back to Van's "What a *dreadful* responsibility" upon winning the Leventritt prize.

After we had greeted the others Van left the table to show us around. With unaffected and somewhat bewildered pride he led us into that second living room, strewn with pictures, books, busts, china, glassware, silver, mementos of every sort from his Russian admirers. As he surveyed them, pointed to them, or fondled them he looked unconvinced. His smile was a tentative question. "Isn't it wonderful?" he whispered, but from his voice you might have gathered that the sheriff was at the door to take everything away.

Three lordly waiters were now wheeling in wagons piled with sizzling platters of steaks, chops, cutlets, and all the trimmings. It was a lavish meal. When it was finished Bill

Judd, as Van's manager, affixed the Cliburn name to the check, adding a suitable tip. Van got up quickly, peered over Judd's shoulder, and turned pale. "Can we *afford* this?" he mumbled. This early in the game he had little conception of his tremendous earning potential.

The afternoon provided a delightful demonstration of the efficacy of the sign language. Since Van and Kondrashin could not really converse—Kondrashin knew as little English then as Van did Russian—they had worked out a two-hand alphabet which apparently satisfied their needs. And of course they expressed musical agreement in the time-honored continental manner. "How do they talk together?" Arthur Hays Sulzberger asked Elliott Sanger next day during a luncheon at the *Times*. Sanger, who had already asked me that question, was armed with the answer: "They don't talk. They embrace." At this, Sulzberger choked on a mouthful of soup.

Van and Kiril had gone straight from the airport to Carnegie Hall that morning to rehearse with the Symphony of the Air for their first concert Monday. Naturally, on the afternoon of our visit hundreds of details required immediate attention, but first "this good and warm man," as Kondrashin calls Van, wanted to make sure that his friend was not stranded. I had meanwhile discovered that Kondrashin spoke fair German, and so with my smattering of Russian and our working knowledge of German, Constance and I offered to take him in hand. It promised to be a lark for us and, we hoped, for him, too.

On our way out he asked us to stop off at his suite, where he presented us with Russian cigarettes—he was smoking American brands which Van had just bought him. He also gave us some of his recordings. As we left he expressed interest in paintings, so we first took him to the home of our friends the Spingolds, where he could see one of the finest private collections of French impressionism in our country. He was keenly responsive and impressively informed.

Afterward we brought him to our apartment. He showed an avid curiosity about the details of our living arrangements. With explorative seriousness he examined every gadget: refrigerator, electric range, air-conditioning units. My electric razor created a sensation; so did the decorative and washable wallpaper in our bathrooms.

Then we settled down for a cup of tea in our den, where he listened intently to the sound of his own records on our phonographic equipment and then to some of our American orchestras and soloists. His gentle hazel eyes and sensitive face lit up with pleasure as passages came through with unaccustomed realism, and his eloquent hands registered his reactions dramatically, with clenched fists or prayerful clasps, a raised index finger or a lowered thumb.

His comments divulged a musical taste that runs in many directions: to opera, to the classical symphonists, and to the creative spirit of our time. A man of simple origins, he feels that great art must be brought to people and belong to all the people; that the artist's strength must be drawn from people and its fruits returned to them through the need of communication. "Just like Vanya," he said.

After dinner we took him to the top of Radio City to view our town at night. As we ascended on that swift, vertical trip to the dizzy height he stiffened visibly and held his breath. When we arrived he peered cautiously over the rails and stared, shaking his head in disbelief. Later, on Broadway, I pointed out the *Time* neon sign with the Van Cliburn cover story advertised in tall letters. When we showed him the blow-up of Van's cover picture from that magazine filling a Doubleday Book Shop window, he was really floored. Not so much because Americans were making such a fuss over Van—after all, nothing could surpass the Russian fuss —but because of our striking methods of display.

We got back to his hotel around midnight, and he insisted on our going up with him for "just a moment." There was some fishing around in the interior of a brief case; then out came a large tin of fresh caviar. (Have you ever tasted fresh caviar just flown over from Russia?) We embraced Kiril and left.

The advance demand for Van's opening concert was the heaviest ever experienced in Carnegie Hall's star-studded history. When no more tickets were available scalpers were asking, and getting, one hundred and fifty dollars a pair. On Monday evening standing-room admissions went on sale at seven-thirty. A lucky handful managed to get them a half hour before concert time at $2.80 apiece. Hundreds were turned away; the house was as tightly packed as the caviar in the tin.

Van's return from his Russian conquests to Carnegie Hall was one of the most harrowing tests any artist has had to face. Confronting a supercharged audience ablaze with curiosity and limp from anticipation, he handled himself superbly, his very entrance establishing him at once as a modest, lovable, and striking personality. With the volcanic applause still echoing around him, he sat down and promptly addressed himself to his prize-winning program. He played it from first to last with an unbelievable absorption and imperturbable control, with courage and calm and admirable restraint. A fervent public responded with unquenchable ovations.

Louis Biancolli articulated the public relief with the statement, "We can all breathe easily now. The Russians were right."

Even before the artist had taken his last bow, there was a concerted rush for backstage. Those who had not come equipped with knee guards and brass knuckles found the trip to the greenroom rugged. Rosina Lhevinne, faced with an early rehearsal next morning, was forced merely to write her congratulations on the face of her program and entrust it for delivery to a sturdier physique.

Another "first" was established that night—the first time in Carnegie Hall's history that the artists' room backstage proved so utterly inadequate that the orchestra's enormous instrument room had to be thrown open to accommodate the mob. Even then photographers had to stand on tables, and attendants tore their hair as Van gave an early demonstration of his handling of crowds. With at least a thousand people squashed in corridors, waiting to shake his hand or ask for an autograph, he engaged in unhurried conversation with all, especially with any teen-ager who appeared to have a serious interest in music: "What do you play? Who is your teacher? What are you studying now?" And he listened to the answers and commented on them. He still had a vivid memory of the days, such a very few years ago, when he had treasured every word gleaned from artists backstage.

Outside the stage door the jam was even worse. The presence of Mayor Wagner had called for a heavy escort of New York's finest. The Mayor himself had left the building quietly, but the officers had been called into action hurriedly when that unmistakable head of hair appeared at the door and the mass attack started. One rookie, arms interlocked with his buddies' in a living chain, sweat beading his forehead, snarled in amazement, "Jeepers, I wouldn't even wish this on me mudder-in-law!"

In the course of the evening's tumult Skitch Henderson caught Vaniel's eye over a sea of faces for a moment and waved: "See you after the war!" Actually, he was to see him the following Sunday on the "Steve Allen Show." How that engagement was booked and how the price was arrived at are well worth detailing, as a demonstration of what head-lines can do to an artist's fees.

The first time Van had played on the "Tonight" show as a Leventritt winner, he was supposed to receive the union minimum of fifty-five dollars. On Henderson's insistence—"Give him seventy-five, *please*"—the ante was raised.

The second time Van played on the show he was paid a hundred dollars. "He did great the last time, and he needs the dough." And by a curious coincidence the date of that appearance was April 13, 1955. Exactly three years later to the day, everything of a sudden had changed. Now every-body wanted him at any price. The producers of the "Steve Allen Show" called Skitch Henderson's apartment. "Can we get that guy?"

Skitch knew what "guy" was meant. He called up Bill Judd. Judd was in no position as yet to make a firm com-mitment, with Van still in Moscow, but Skitch was satisfied with a gentleman's understanding: "Just give me your word."

That was sufficient. At midday the Ed Sullivan office was on the hook, requesting the same segment of time on the very same date. Sorry, there's an option. . . .

By the time offices opened on Monday, Judd had been able to clear the matter long-distance with Van, who said that so far he'd thought of only two such appearances after he returned—one on TV with Skitch and one on radio with me, for old times' sake.

Skitch and Judd agreed that Van should do the final movement of the Tchaikovsky Concerto and that film clips should be shown from the Moscow competition. "All right, then," said Skitch, "we're all fixed up except for settling with the money man."

The money man called. How much?

"Three thousand."

"*What?*"

"Three thousand." Dollars.

A very long pause. "Okay, we'll send a check."

In no time *this* was to be peanuts.

10

Tall at the Keyboard

Philadelphia and Washington were also impatient to hear the prize-winning program and to judge for themselves if "the Russians were right." No less did they want to see Van and to honor him. At the last moment the National Association of Concert Managers switched their annual convention to the nation's capital where they could attend the Washington concert.

The rabid public curiosity posed the problem of how best to travel. Van's unique appearance—Rosalie Berner calls him "my friend from Mars"—causes crowds to surround him at sight. Putting him on a train would be sheer homicide unless no other transportation was available. This time it was. Two air-conditioned Cadillacs were rented, and the Cliburn caravan started for Philadelphia the day after the ticker-tape event.

In the front seat of the first car rode the chauffeur, F. C. Schang, and Kondrashin, who likes to be where he can get a good view. In the back were Mr. and Mrs. Cliburn, Rich-

ard Murphy, music editor of *Time,* and his researcher, Rose-
marie Tauris. And mountains of luggage. In the front seat
of the second car rode the chauffeur; Elizabeth Winston,
Van's press representative; and manager Judd. In the back
with Van was magazine writer Stanley Frank, who lugged
a portable tape recorder. They worked all the way to Philly,
their only chance of completing the interview.

Weaving through the mid-town traffic of both cities took
most of the traveling time; the rest was a breeze. The clocks
were striking five when the two cars entered the precincts of
Brotherly Love. A press conference, however, had been
called at the Hotel Warwick for one-thirty. Nevertheless, as
the second car passed a Howard Johnson soda emporium
Van yelled "Stop!" and got out to buy himself a strawberry
ice cream cone, triple scoop.

Shortly after, it was apparent that the chauffeur had taken
a wrong turn—the hotel was over on the other side of the
square. "Let's get out and walk." On the way Van spotted
a church. "Let's go inside." To the infinite relief of his press
aide, who by now was chewing her fingernails to the wrist,
the doors were locked. So across to the hotel; a moment's
pause to finish off the cone; and now into the lobby with
the old boyish bounce.

Mother and Father Cliburn had arrived at the Warwick
a half hour before, hungry and exhausted, and had gone up-
stairs to their rooms. And what a reception greeted them as
they stepped across the threshold of their suite! Head on
into a battery of TV cameras, photographer's flash bulbs,
radio equipment, and the assembled ladies and gentlemen
of the working press—that is, if they also work who only
stand and wait. These had been waiting, if not standing,
about the length of a double-feature movie. Downstairs sat

Sidney Fields, who was not unamused at having traveled to another city to get material from a resident of New York for a series of Cliburn articles appearing in the *New York Mirror*.

It was decided to pen Van up with Fields first, in a corner of the downstairs restaurant, and hold the others at bay. They waited. The waitresses were also waiting . . . to waylay Van. Just a word, just an autograph. Just a touch of the fingers, the hem of the robe.

The next day Van thought he ought to buy some clothes —at least a raincoat and tweed jacket. His appearance in Wanamaker's department store nearly incited a riot. People ran around like the denizens of an ant hill suddenly kicked open. "Van Cliburn is here!" they shrilled to each other. "*You* know!" One old gentleman almost fell off the escalator leaning out to tremolo, "God bless you, son! Bless you always for what you did for America!"

Trying to replenish his meager wardrobe or, in fact, doing any sort of shopping was getting to be a real problem. His clothes were being worn and torn to shreds. I had seen Paul Moor's description in *Time* of his outfit in Russia: "a single dress shirt, a plastic wing collar given to him by a friend, a ratty grey Shetland sweater that often showed under his dress jacket when he took his bows." I hoped it was perhaps a bit exaggerated. It wasn't.

That I discovered just before his second New York appearance when he laughingly called to my attention that the sole of his right shoe was flapping. When I asked why he wore it he answered that these were his only shoes, that he'd had no time to buy new ones or to send these out to be mended. He nearly broke his neck with them at Carnegie Hall and at the Mayor's luncheon.

"Carnegie!" I echoed. "But how *could* you take such a chance at the concert? How could you pedal?"

"Oh," he winked, "I just slipped a rubber band over the toe. It held fine."

The day after the Philadelphia concert—so howling a triumph that the fans tore the handle off one of the Cadillacs as it drove from the hall—the Gypsy Caravan, as Van began to call it, divided in half. The first Cadillac headed back to Gotham, bearing the *Time* personnel. The second headed for Washington with the driver and Kondrashin in the front with some of the luggage; Mother, Miss Winston, and Van in the back—with his long legs jackknifed to leave room for Father Cliburn and Bill Judd, who perched on the jump seats. Even with the air conditioning the heat soon became so intolerable that the party dissolved into that laughing, helpless hysteria which makes misery bearable and awfully funny in retrospect.

At two in the morning they rolled into Washington, cramped and ravenous. The hotel dining room was closed; no room service till morning (ah, the glamorous life of the touring troubadour!). While the others went to bed unfed, Van dragged Liz Winston and the chauffeur around until they found an all-night snack bar that served hamburgers and coffee. There a pianist from a night club took one quick look and moved over to unreel his life story. Van listened avidly. With all eternity at disposal when talking to people, Van even asked for a few missing details. At last they all called it a day and walked back to the hotel. A few hours' sleep, and then to the White House.

Van insisted on taking Kondrashin and his parents with him to see President Eisenhower. After all, as Russia's honored guest he had learned to become very comfortable around heads of state. They were welcomed by Sherman Adams and James C. Hagerty and taken directly to the Chief Executive's office, for he was about to take off by helicopter for his Gettysburg farm. He greeted them cordially, and, as one Texan to others, the President proudly showed them some family pictures.

Unfortunately, the President was not to attend the concert that evening; nor would Mrs. Eisenhower, who had already left for the weekend; nor Vice-President Nixon, who had just returned from a "good-will tour" of South America. But the President was sure Van would have no trouble with his concert appearances in this country "after coming out on top in that kind of ordeal over there."

The working press was curious: "Did the President congratulate you on winning the contest?" Van was asked afterward.

"Yes, I think so," he answered evenly. "I think he did it eliptically, if nothing else."

From the Executive Mansion they all went to a luncheon given by the Texas delegation, attended by many of the Cliburns' old friends. Gold cuff links had been designed to express the Lone Star's joy in "Texas' proudest brag": the motif comprised the opening phrase of the Tchaikovsky First. To enhance Van's enjoyment an identical pair had been made for Kondrashin.

Constitution Hall that night presented one of the most glamorous and glittering spectacles of many seasons. The elite of Washington was out in full force. In Russian Ambassador Menshikov's box the elder Cliburns sat in state. Backstage everyone was staggered by the giant basket of flowers sent by Menshikov, conveying his good wishes for the greatest success to artist and maestro.

An exclusive gourmet supper to honor artists after a concert is still in the finest European tradition. That night the Soviet Embassy served supper for fifty. Van and Kondrashin sat at the head of the horseshoe table with Ambassador and Mme. Menshikov; and the first-desk men of the orchestra were among the honored guests. Toast followed toast every few minutes, each plate ringed with five glasses for champagne, brandy, a choice of vintage wines, and vodka from the source. Mme. Menshikov saw that Mrs. Cliburn did not drink alcohol and taught her in a charmingly inconspicuous manner how to "pretend" on the toasts without being detected. It was all sumptuous, expansive, and glowing with good-neighbor amity. At the end of it Van spontaneously went to the piano and played, on and on.

Once again music invoked its magic power to banish differences. The atmosphere grew ever warmer and gayer, and Elizabeth Winston caught a new slant on the effects of TV on language. Introducing herself to a Russian gentleman, she spoke very clearly and slowly to help him understand. "My name is E-liz-a-beth Win-ston," she enunciated distinctly, "W-i-n-s-t-o-n."

His face lit up instantly. "Yes," he said archly. "Like a cigarette should!"

The following day Van vanished in the direction of Mount Vernon with an escort of Texans, back in time for the annual dinner of the White House correspondents. Here, among so many distinguished participants, he was given first place on the program, since he had to fly back to Manhattan as soon as possible.

Although Van has never been caught making a note for a speech he is rarely at a loss for an effective opener. "Brother Sam," he called out across the tundras of tables. "Are you out there somewhere? Won't you please stand up?" And the Speaker of the House arose to receive a gale of applause whistled up by a youngster who wasn't even born when his grandpa served with Mr. Rayburn in the Texas legislature. As Skitch Henderson has suggested: "Vaniel would probably have been a success at anything, even if he'd stayed down in Texas and gone into the oil business."

Saturday night they all flew back to New York; even Bill Judd, who loathes being higher than a skyscraper. Schuyler Chapin was on hand to meet them when they landed at Newark. None of them had eaten anything except a stale box-lunch hurried aboard the plane, so they wound up at Sardi's. As they walked in Leonard Lyons spotted them; then other night-souls gathered about like moths around a light. Van held court for the next couple of hours.

When they returned to the Pierre he was still so keyed up he knew he couldn't sleep, so he begged them to come into his suite and talk. Every so often Dad Cliburn would shuffle in from his bedroom, rubbing his eyes. "You've *got* to let this poor boy have some sleep," he'd scold at Liz Winston and Bill Judd. They'd agree wholeheartedly. "By now," says Liz Winston, "we needed toothpicks to prop up our eyelids." But as soon as they tried to leave, Van would snatch at them pathetically. "Oh, please. *Please* don't go. Not yet. Let's have just another cigarette." They talked until dawn.

"In that first hectic period after Van got home from Russia," Liz Winston records, "I lost thirteen pounds. Bill Judd lost eight. Kondrashin got real thin, and of course Van was a scarecrow." However, Van had his arsenal of vitamins, his fortress of youth, and that spiritual energy which sustains the thrice-blessed.

The second of his Carnegie concerts, that Monday evening, was broadcast over WQXR. We got together in the afternoon over a microphone to tape an informal public chat to be heard during intermission, and we covered a wide range of subjects. Then I popped The Question.

"What are your plans generally for acquiring the time, the privacy for reflection, for doing the kind of work every true artist does and never stops doing?"

"Well, Abram," he answered slowly, "I have certainly not had much time to sit down and think. As I've often said to my manager, 'I wonder how long Van Cliburn will be able to go on without practicing.'"

This didn't quite answer my question, but it showed that even then he was fully aware of his problem.

Late that night, as we all sat around in his hotel suite, the stupendous ovation still roaring in our ears, we discussed the matter more fully. "First things must come first," we concluded. But what should come first among so many equals, remained the question.

Food and soft drinks had been sent up from downstairs, and Van by now was signing the checks with an ingratiating flourish. At three, guests began to leave. I had noticed that the Cliburns were so busy being hosts that they had merely nibbled at a quarter of a sandwich apiece, washed down by a glass or two of club soda. So I said, "I'll bet you're all starved. How about going to Reuben's for a bite?"

Van and his mother grew almost emotional over the idea. Dad Cliburn gave me a tired, resigned smile. "You-all go along," he said in his pure Texan, "I'm *daid*."

Late as it was, our short walk down was like a royal procession. Cab drivers saluted with their horns and waved. Policemen slapped Van on the back, doormen pumped his arm and thanked him in the now-familiar phrase "for doing what you did for us over there." When we entered the restaurant, surely one of the most celebrity-hardened places in the city, the sixty-odd awestruck customers craned, nudged, and let out little shrieks of glee.

On the way to our table we passed a convivial party of three gentlemen of somewhat dubious distinction. One rose unsteadily and reached out for Van's hand. Van shook it warmly as the drunk, overcome, slid to the floor. Van helped him up with the tenderness of a mother lifting a babe from a crib and put him back on his chair. The poor man, racked with shame and remorse, began to blubber his appreciation and congratulations. Van pulled a chair up from an adjoining table and put his arm around the humiliated man and said, "Do you *really* mean it? Did I do *that* much?"

I looked around to see if anyone else had observed the incident. They all had. Never have I seen so many after-midnight faces in Manhattan so shining with warmth.

To how many are such opportunities given in this tough world? There is no doubt that Van assumed his new role in life quite naturally. It was not only deeply rewarding in a serious way, but it also enabled him to enjoy himself hugely on every level of extravagant giving. He went to Tiffany's to buy a silver table service for Kondrashin's child and on the way back stepped into Schwarz's and bought the little one a mammoth Russian bear costing seventy-five dollars. Each time he first chose the gift and only later asked the price. He took friends to luxurious restaurants and grabbed large checks, all in candid, uproarious merriment at the spectacle of Van Cliburn, of all people, spending in a flash and on one spree what formerly would have carried him through a month of total living.

Occasionally, however, he would catch himself in the act of being "taken" and would revert to type with indignation. On our way to visit a mutual friend we stopped at a florist's, and Van selected two small bunches of spring flowers. The florist obviously recognized his customer at sight, and after he had wrapped the tiny bouquets he announced: "That will be ten dollars plux tax." Van inhaled sharply. "Ten dollars!" he exclaimed, and looked around not knowing quite what to do. I chimed in, "It's outrageous, Van. What do you say, let's leave them?" Van surveyed the situation with a frown. "I'll take one bunch," he decided. It was hard to tell who was more infuriated, Van or the florist, who had to unwrap and then rewrap the purchase.

On Decoration Day, Van was visited by Ed Murrow on "Person to Person." On Sunday, Mother was also a TV guest on "What's My Line?" The day between, Van drove in an open convertible to Rachmaninoff's grave at Valhalla, New York, to plant the bush he had brought from Russia. The lean, lanky pianist was at the wheel, all six-foot-four of him, and he stuck out of the car like a pink dogwood in bloom. Instantly the highway became filled with sounds of honking horns and jubilant cries of "Hi, Van!" from adults wreathed in smiles and from children who leaned out dangerously to wave at their new hero. He always responded with a shy grin while he fanned the air with fingers that Winthrop Sargeant describes as "a bunch of asparagus."

That was also the day he acquired a gold talisman second only in importance to the Moscow medal—the small Czar Nicholas coin which Rachmaninoff always carried around for luck. It was presented to Van by the composer's daughter, Princess Irena Wolkonsky, during the ceremonies.

Back at the hotel suite telegrams and fan mail by now

were leaning in crazy stacks atop tables and dressers, filling cartons and drawers, spilling off every flat surface. Van groaned whenever he returned to the apartment. But something had to be done immediately with the souvenirs and presents from Russia, many of them beyond price.

Van appealed to Frederick Steinway. Could he find room at the Steinway building to store it all? Gladly, said Steinway, if Van would permit them to exhibit it. Gladly, said Van. Thereupon Frederick Steinway and Schuyler Chapin spent the next few days supervising the packing and transporting of many huge boxes from the Pierre to the Steinway showrooms, where display cases were filled with some twenty-five hundred items of what became one of the most fascinating exhibits in the city. When Van saw it his first thought was of Alexander Greiner, who had died while he was in Russia. "The thing that hurts me most is that I never did get to see him after I had won."

The Cliburn collection will be on loan exhibition for an indeterminate time. It should be seen. Apart from its intrinsic allurement, it constitutes the whole treasure-trove of the Russian people's affection for an American boy.

Van could no longer keep his harvest with him because he was moving out of the Pierre, and his old quarters on Fifty-seventh Street, which he still used as a hideaway, seemed inadequate. He asked friends about town to help him find a larger place. But nothing came of all the scouting and hunting. Even though he was Van Cliburn, he was still a pianist—the bête noire of Manhattan landlords.

It mattered little to Van. Besides, he'd be home so rarely. Within a month of his return from Moscow he was off again for England and the Continent. London, Amsterdam, Brussels, Paris—all had snared him and his "prize-winning program." But the bouquet this time was that he took his parents with him—to Europe! This, after all his mother's hard work and his father's labor and planning and saving, was the paramount prize he had yet gathered. He had said to me in those first early days, "Thank God, now I can give Mama everything, so that she never has to work again unless she wants to. And Daddy, too." Then he had been talking of security. Now it was much more than that: it was the American dream of being able to "see the world."

Mr. Cliburn, in his lovable, self-effacing way, came into his own. In Britain he traced his family tree, to find that the name Cliburn comes from Claiborne. His American progenitor was William Claiborne, who sailed to Virginia as a surveyor in 1621, remained to lead two expeditions against the Indians, and later was appointed treasurer of the colony for life.

In Amsterdam, Papa Cliburn found a fellow spirit and a fellow Rotarian. Having broken the clasp on his Rotary pin, he was a little concerned because the thing wouldn't stay on properly. "Here," said Prince Bernhard, royal consort to Queen Juliana of the Netherlands, "you can't go around like that." And so saying, he took off his own Rotary emblem and fastened it fraternally to his guest's lapel.

Russia was not on Van's itinerary, nor was it when he again returned to Europe two months later. He afterward announced plans for a two-and-a-half-months' tour of the Soviet Union in the spring of 1959, but an infected finger in February forced him to cancel all work for the time.

11

A Prophet and a Profit
in His Own Country

Van's main thread of interest, as we have seen, was anything but money for its own sweet sake. But his glimpse of adversity before Moscow and his limitless opportunities after forcibly compelled him to face the stark realities of his environment—the environment of the material world in which men are appraised by what they get from it, not what they give to it.

A long time had elapsed since Van had been paid his topmost fee of one thousand dollars. With the news from Russia, while Van was still abroad, the concert fee jumped to twenty-five hundred, except for the few dates already booked before he left. All would be honored at the prices originally agreed upon. Van, who never forgets those who stuck with him, was "delighted to play them."

In Chicago a subhead in the August issue of *Musical Leader* read: "Congratulations to Manager Walter L. Larsen on Your Foresight." Foresight indeed. "A throng of 70,000 sat in awed silence" at the first of the two outdoor concerts in Grant Park; the same at the second. Manager Larsen had paid $800 for the *two*. Admission is free. Not only was there no hint of complaint from Van, but he found the air "just electrified" and declared that the vibrations and rapport he felt between himself and his audiences was more like Russia than anything he had experienced since his return. The huge public did its best to reciprocate. Several hundred policemen had to keep him from being crushed to death.

In the hotel lobby the teen-agers were waiting, still exultant after a vigil of hours. Before Van left town he was informed that the Elvis Presley Fan Club of Chicago had changed its name to the Van Cliburn Fan Club. From American youth this was at least the Tchaikovsky Gold Medal all over again.

At the Hollywood Bowl the advance announcement cleaned out the twenty-thousand seats two nights running, but this was not for free as at Grant Park. Van, prone to doubt, was now fully converted to his unprecedented drawing power. If big money was to be made on him, he felt the fairness of insisting upon his just share. He wanted $18,000 for these two evenings, and he got it. And from now on there would be less talk of fees and more of grosses and percentages.

Still, with a childlike charm he described his personal experiences in the garrison of glamour. What thrilled him was to sup with Danny Kaye, visit with Jack Benny, practice in the home of the late Cecil B. De Mille, and to find himself the favorite of the movie stars who had always been *his* favorites. Not a word did he mention of the concerts or of their prodigious success.

At Lewisohn Stadium, a larger-than-usual deficit loomed, due to rains and cancellations. But the man from Mars was coming on his white and black charger. It was decided to schedule the Van Cliburn concert as a post-season event. As soon as the posters went up the Stadium was sold out . . . and how. Tables for eight became tables for twelve; the regular admission scale of thirty cents to three dollars became one to five dollars. Van's fee was doubled to five thousand, yet Minnie Guggenheimer (Mrs. Stadium) rejoiced. "*This*," she said, "is music to my ears." The concert wasn't to be played until the next night.

Constance and I went up for the rehearsal. During intermission we went backstage to find the devoted "Benny"— Bernard Mulryan, who for over thirty years has been the artists' friend in their darkest hours of need at Carnegie and the Stadium—hovering over Van. "Are you bundled up? You mustn't catch cold," Benny warned. Then: "Did you bring an extra shirt? Remember last time: you got all sweated up. And remember, you're going out to a party after the concert."

As we chatted Van turned suddenly: "Connie," he said, "I did something last week I've wanted to do all my life."

"What was that, Van?"

"Well, I rented a gorgeous Lincoln Continental, snow-white and baby-blue. I rode all over the place all week with the top down. But it cost *ninety* dollars! For one week! Do you think I was wicked to spend all that money?"

We laughed.

"But really, it's the first thing I've done for myself. Now

that I've got it out of my system I won't have to do it again. But what a thrill it was!"

This from a young man whose intimates have seen him turn down, without a second of hesitation, movie offers and TV appearances that would have surely amounted to half a million dollars. He has consistently refused to exploit his success in any but the most legitimate and dignified manner. But he did admit, rather wistfully, "I will confess that the old stage pull returned, and I wavered a bit before rejecting the opportunity to act and play in a movie. It's impossible now, of course, but it's fine for character building when one must sacrifice minor ambitions for primary responsibilities."

To date he has put out only one recording, the Tchaikovsky. Yet, reported *Variety*, "The platter by the Texas pianist . . . is now expected to hit the 1,000,000 marker by the end of the year . . . the first time that a longhair artist has come up with a million-seller on an individual disk." It is gratifying to Van, but it is no reason, as he sees it, for him to put out any record that doesn't satisfy him artistically.

With all this gold showering in I asked him jokingly at dinner one evening, "Well, what's the status now—rich man, poor man, Indian chief?"

"Abram," he replied, "I've got one hundred dollars in the bank." He meant, of course, his personal account. "Money men," lawyers, accountants, personal representatives had all been attached to the Cliburn entourage ever since he became Big Business. They've been telling him what's what.

"My advisers tell me so many people are making money out of me," he said, shaking his head. Nor did he know the half of it. Down in Kilgore, Texas, even the little girl next door was in the act. Requested to raise some money for her Brownie troop, she was discovered by her mother one day permitting the neighborhood kids to come in and sit on "Van Cliburn's fence," the common boundary between the two yards. The eight-year-old entrepreneur was charging a quarter admission.

Meanwhile, the poor little rich boy hardly had the time to spend a quarter on himself. He did acquire a fine Sheraton secretary and a richly covered *bergère* for his tiny apartment. But still no wardrobe to speak of. He showed up at our home one night a trifle tardy for dinner. "I ran all over town," he apologized, "trying to find a shoe store open. You know, I still have only one pair of shoes, the ones I bought to replace the flapping sole. These aren't flapping yet, but I do wish I could find time to buy some others."

At his apartment a few days later he was dressing for an important luncheon. I saw him reach for a black tie that lay coiled on the dresser. It looked more like a shoestring. "Van," I ventured as tactfully as possible, "could I find you another?"

"It's an old friend, Abram," he protested. "I *love* it." I felt as though I had impugned some family heirloom.

New York was awfully hot, and Constance had lined up three friends with swimming pools and arranged for some quiet swimming parties she thought Van would enjoy. "Oh, marvelous," he said. But the very next morning after the Stadium concert he popped up at Elizabeth Winston's office. "I'm off for Washington," he announced. "Going right to Idlewild now." He was due to leave shortly for Brussels to play the World's Fair again, at the Soviet Pavilion. Whatever he had in mind, he was off to see our State Department about it first.

On his return a few days later I noticed a slight change from his old jaunty attitude; some of the first-bloom confidence had powdered off. The visit he clouded in mystery, except to say that he ran around without getting anywhere. I formed my own conclusions from a news release in the stiff-necked phraseology of diplomacy:

> Washington, Aug. 9. Van Cliburn has the State Department's permission for performances next week-end with a Russian Symphony orchestra in Brussels and Ostend, Belgium.
>
> Officials here said that it was not up to them to say whether a concert artist could perform . . . They said only that the United States had no objection to his playing at the commercial concerts.

What Van had hoped for, I suspect, was some sort of official blessing, some "arms-across-the-sea" gesture. Instead came the cold, tacit no-objection. Apparently, our administration was still being slow to avail itself of the tremendous popularity and inherent value of our artists abroad despite the many lessons to be learned—the most recent from the enthusiastic welcome which Leonard Bernstein and Dimitri Mitropoulos had won with the Philharmonic in the identical Latin-American cities where they followed in the footsteps of Vice-President Nixon's ill-starred journey.

Without benefit of officialdom Van fulfilled his Russian-Belgian commitments; then, without fanfare, played for our servicemen in Heidelberg. The Army flew him back to Washington; the Navy flew him to New York; a taxi took him home to another thousand messages, a long list of concerts, and the same waiting Steinway.

On the way back Van had done some hard thinking. "When I travel on planes or trains," he once told me, "I can think best about what I'm going to do in the future." He had worked out one gracious public gesture and one long-term public plan. Before the month was over he had put them both into action.

At a press conference held in Steinway Hall he announced that he was giving a check for twelve hundred and fifty dollars to the New York City Department of Commerce and Public Events to use at its discretion for the cultural benefit of the city. The gift, half of the prize money he was able to take out of Russia, had first been offered to the Martha Baird Rockefeller Aid to Music Program, Van said, in appreciation of the thousand dollars he had received for his trip over. Mrs. Rockefeller had thankfully declined. In the same spirit of gratitude he was giving the money to the city. It was gratefully accepted on behalf of Mayor Wagner by Robert Dowling and Assistant Commissioner Rothblatt.

The second announcement concerned his decision to open his rehearsals to teen-agers. In Leningrad he had requested that students be admitted during preparatory sessions with the orchestra. In New York he had invited a group of students who had been unable to get into his concerts to the recording sessions of the Tchaikovsky. He loved having these young people around him. Over and over he has said "After all, they are my contemporaries, with just a few years' difference." One realizes it with something of a start, for Van is such an "old soul" in so many ways, it is easy to forget his extreme youth.

Although the teen-age plan had been brewing in his mind for some time, its immediate stimulus was a letter received by columnist Cedric Adams of the *Minneapolis Star* from young Lolita Ehle. She wrote shortly before Van was to appear in the Twin Cities: "Don't you think it might be possible for a concert—probably a matinée—to be given for the young people of our Upper Midwest somewhat tailored to the budgets of teen-agers? . . . There have been lots of indictments against teen-agers and their alleged yen for rock 'n' roll. This could be a sort of mass demonstration that we also have a cultural side. And I feel sure that Van Cliburn would bend a willing ear to an appeal if it were only made to him."

Mr. Adams saw that it was. The first teen-age concert was staged in New Haven on September 29 when the Pied Piper of the Piano played the Schumann and Rachmaninoff Third concertos with Frank Brieff conducting. At fifty cents a head the hall was packed solidly, and hundreds were turned away. A letter to Van from two fans tells its own story:

> Dear Mr. Cliburn:
>
> My girl friend and I would just like to take this opportunity to thank you for your wonderful thoughtfulness.
>
> We were just 2 of the thousands of teen-agers that jammed Woolsey Hall to see you and hear you play. We would never have been able to afford the regular prices, and we wanted very much to see you.
>
> I don't know whether or not you know this, but your idea was such a big success, that it has been adopted for all time to come . . . Thank you again Mr. Cliburn from the bottom of our hearts.
>
> Your fans always, etc.

The second event, at Scarsdale, New York, brought out eighteen hundred youngsters in spite of an icy autumn rain, and seven puzzled policemen were assigned to keep order. "For Elvis, I could understand it," one said to a reporter.

"But for this crowd to sit quiet and listen to Van Cliburn play it straight—this is a revelation."

And this is the way it has gone all over the country. Moppets who knew a jukebox tune called "Tonight We Love" but had never heard of Tchaikovsky sat with respectful attention and listened and learned . . . and loved it. A few sophisticates showed up and showed off with printed scores. The terms of admission were left to the judgments and necessities of the individual orchestras and school boards, but in every situation Van has asked that if admission could not be free the price should at least be kept to a minimum.

Of course, all of this imposes more strain upon Van. Rehearsals with audiences present are still performances of a sort. And then there are those autographing assemblies. . . .

Van's hardest day and largest concert income from dawn to dusk came in Austin, where he was originally booked to play one matinée performance as the centerpiece of the University of Texas' Festival of Fine Arts. The clamor for tickets, however, was so far-reaching that the schedule had to be augmented. Van motored into town that Sunday morning of November 23, after a swing through Arkansas and a quick stopover at Kilgore. With only an hour's sleep he did his morning dress rehearsal before a gym full of school children and university students who paid a half dollar each for the treat. That afternoon he played the scheduled concert to an audience of 7000, at five o'clock to another 4000. He went through it in "finest fettle," according to all accounts. Afterward he was made an "Admiral of the Texas Navy." For this one-day "festival" his accumulated fees were $10,500. A fair return for a day's work.

Two weeks before, in Waco, Texas, the giving and taking had been conversely modulated. Booked to play Baylor University as the crowning feature of its Conference on American Ideals, he had been offered an honorary degree. He had told us about it in advance. "What d'you think?" he'd exclaimed one night as we rode in a taxi. "Baylor University wants to give me a doctorate! Can you imagine? It's not as strange as it sounds, though. The degree is in humanities, not in music, and it's really not because of me. Did you know my great-grandfather was a founder of Baylor, and its first president?" He said he would be honored to accept it, but he did not reveal what he had up his sleeve. We learned about that from the newspapers.

At the end of the concert Dr. W. R. White, president of Baylor, announced that Van Cliburn wished to make some endowments to the university: in memory of great-grandfather Solomon Green O'Bryan, one thousand dollars to the Department of Religion; in memory of grandfather William Carey O'Bryan, one thousand to the School of Law; in memory of grandmother Sirilda McClain O'Bryan, a thousand to the Drama Department; in living memory of mother Rildia O'Bryan Cliburn, another thousand to the School of Music.

A splendid surprise! It had merely been known to the inner circle that Van had planned to return the four-thousand-dollar fee for his services as soloist with the Baylor University Symphony Orchestra, conducted by Dean Daniel Sternberg. But a startling climax was yet to come with Dr. White's final announcement that, additionally, Van and his father were jointly donating ten thousand dollars to establish a fund for the university orchestra. Fourteen thousand dollars presented at one fell swoop; a four-thousand-dollar fee gracefully declined.

Another day's work; another kind of profit. And still

another has been the contribution of his services with orchestras for the benefit of their pension funds. The scramble for seats at the highest prices ever charged for such concerts has demonstrated that Cliburn's ability to render tangible aid to fellow musicians has never been equaled. In Boston the response so exceeded the capacity of Symphony Hall that for the first time in that orchestra's venerable history a repeat concert was staged and solidly sold out the very next night. Four months prior to a similar event for the welfare of the New York Philharmonic, a ticket was the scarcest item in town, at any price. In Philadelphia, with Maria Meneghini Callas as co-star and admission scaled up to $200 per, nearly two hundred thousand dollars poured into the box office for the celebration of the 102nd anniversary of the Academy of Music.

It is good to know that a prophet who so profits others has not remained without honor in his own country.

12

In the Lions' Cage

The surest proof that a personality has become a legend lies in the re-emergence of stories, tarnished with age, which are polished anew and pinned on the current hero. The most common Cliburn story that went the rounds at every gathering and spread like wildfire through the country was the one about the Texan who climbed into his private plane to attend Van's first Carnegie appearance after Moscow. The stranger to New York landed at La Guardia Airport and approached the first lady he saw. "Ma'am," he inquired, lifting his ten-gallon hat, "could you tell me how I can get to Carnegie Hall?" The lady surveyed him coldly and answered, "Yes. You must practice, practice, practice."

Another proof appears when one, without being named, becomes the point of a TV witticism, as in Victor Borge's laugh-provoking crack: "Tchaikovsky was born in 1840 and was a rather obscure musician until 1958 when he was discovered by a Texan." Or when one becomes "18 across" and "4 down" in a *Times* crossword puzzle. And even, or perhaps particularly, when one becomes the subject of a shockingly scurrilous and green-eyed poem which was actually circulated through the mails to thousands of musicians, suggesting that the Moscow contest was rigged.

Van takes everything in stride; the jokes and the brickbats, the wangling and maneuvering which surround celebrities. He is besieged from all sides, no matter what he does or where he travels. His days are a dizzy round of practice, rehearsals, and performances; of press interviews, business conferences, professional and social obligations; of autographing pictures, programs, and record albums; and of meals eaten at ridiculous hours. He stays up half the night or all night. Sometimes he practices until 5 or 6 or 7 A.M. and the following day will give a typically vital performance and add a veritable recital of encores. He once told me casually, "You know, I haven't slept two nights in succession for almost two months." I would not have believed anyone else, but I believed him, for I have never known any human body that could take the punishment Cliburn visits on himself and which is visited upon him. It is as Josef Hofmann once said: "When you're obscure, the world starves you to death. When you're famous, the world works you to death."

The matter of effecting a meeting with him or of having him return a telephone call is almost insurmountable. Both his press representative and his management have called his friends to inquire whether they'd been in touch with Van, in despair at not having heard from him in days or even weeks. He has torn his phone out. Messages can be left at the switchboard of his apartment house, but few of them, no matter how urgent, are attended to promptly, if indeed at all. There are just too many.

This has led to some marked asperity on the part of

friends, colleagues, and newspapermen who fail to understand the dilemma. One syndicated column complained:

> Musical New York is talking about the transforma-
> tion in the young man since his summer-long binge of
> celebrity. He has acquired a personal representative and
> other appurtenances of fame, such as not answering the
> telephone, or returning calls to some who were loyal
> to him long before Moscow.

Loyalty or reciprocal loyalty is not quite the point. Even
the parents of this devoted son were soon lamenting the
scarcity of a word from Van. Here, Frederick Steinway came
to the rescue. He had a stationer make up a box entitled
The Van Cliburn Do-It-Yourself Kit. Inside were post cards,
an ink pad, and two rubber stamps. One bore the name and
address of his parents in Kilgore; the other bore the message:

> Dear Mother and Daddy: Everything is all right. I
> love you very much.
>
> Van

This was a gay solution to the problem. As for the other
problems within the lions' cage, there is no solution except
oblivion. A simple stroll up the avenue for a bit of air and
exercise turned into an enormous block party one afternoon. Van was mobbed every step of the way by gaping
fans, autograph seekers, shopkeepers and customers who
streamed out of stores to pump his hand. A bus driver spied
him, applied the brakes violently, and shouted, "There's our
boy!" as passengers waved and squealed greetings while they
struggled to regain their balance.

In an effort to escape for a while, Van turned down a
side street. Within a few blocks he shook off most of his

pursuers and walked into a little out-of-the-way restaurant, smack into the middle of a wedding ceremony. The scene was abruptly converted into a Marx Brothers film sequence when the rabbi caught sight of Van, left the startled bridal couple at the altar, rushed up with the marriage certificate in hand, and thrust it into the unexpected guest's palm, urging him on with excited little cries to sign it.

Van was charmed and charming. He always seems to have the extraordinary faculty of giving himself wholly and without effort. We were dining at the Forum of the Twelve Caesars when a man came up to the table. He told Van he was from Virginia and that he had a gifted young daughter who hated to practice. If Van would autograph the menu it would serve as such an inspiration. Van began to write, his brows tightly knit. He wrote on and on, covering all the pages of that magnificent menu. Before he handed it over I asked to see it. Instead of some formal message of good wishes, Van had poured his heart out to the child, relating how hard he had practiced but how much music meant to him now and would mean to her. He begged her seriously to fulfill her talent which the Lord had given and added that when he came down her way would she give him the pleasure of hearing her play? When we left, hours later, the father was standing in the corner, his eyes just following Van.

It was another instance of Van's you-attitude. He not only receives but reacts. He's a listener as well as a talker. It comes as a shock to those who merely expect to be spectators along the path of his feverish life to find themselves being swept along, carried forward by the man's encircling warmth.

Cliburn's appeal individually and totally has deep roots,

for it bears more than an indirect relationship to the critical world climate around him. No need of our time is more challenging than the peaceful solution to the problems of our swift-moving and frightening universe. Unless the challenge is successfully met, none of us can live in any security or serenity, if indeed we can survive at all.

People everywhere see the old game of power politics being played, only this time with nuclear weapons. They want to put an end to this stupid, senseless business. They are filled with dismay over the disintegration of human relationships through the failures of nuclear diplomacy. They want desperately to reach each other, find each other, articulate their common hopes and interests, calm each other's fears, and assure each other of their essential friendliness.

The artist, at present, is their most eloquent spokesman. The spontaneous and persistent ovations which have greeted Russian artists here, and likewise have greeted our artists in Russia and in satellite countries, were undeniable testimonies to supreme artistry. But the supercharged emotionalism that characterized these occasions has also expressed the profound hope of people for harmonious concord. The Russians say to us through their response to our artists what we say to them reciprocally: "Let us be friends. Let our common love for art help us to understand each other and to live together."

These demonstrations reached their apex with Van's triumph. In Russia and in America, in Belgium and in Holland, in France and in England—apart from acclaiming the pianist—it was apparent that people were trying to tell him something, something he could perhaps tell others whose ear he commands and who matter greatly in this volatile world. All this has helped to weave the Cliburn legend.

People of all kinds and all ages flock about him everywhere. Painters want to paint him, sculptors want to make busts of him. I received a telephone call from a sculptress who had seen Van in Sardi's the day before. She had just "flipped over those marvelous huge hands of his." How could she get him to pose for her? "Oh," I said airily, "it's a cinch. Nothing to it. Just find him and gas him."

If she ever does get to him I'm certain that he will be far more gracious than I was. To everyone he meets personally, he dispenses infinite attentiveness, advice, praise, sympathy —all with an enkindling friendliness. One girl came away from a few words with him looking like one possessed, exclaiming, "Van has doubled my strength!" And though this drains him physically, he cannot be said to be squandering his energies, because in distributing inspiration he too is doubly strengthened.

Distinguished men and women in their own fields, college presidents and government officials—all listen to him with more than deference and hang on every word of this man who evidently knows the secret of nourishing trust and love in others. Van, who by nature has an even greater desire to be loved as a person than admired as a musician, has discovered that this power of love is not only the direct approach to God and to art but also to people.

He takes his strength and his love to the platform, to distribute them en masse. I noticed this particularly during his four October appearances with the New York Philharmonic. An account of this period will give the reader a characteristic vignette of the man against the background of his turbulent concert life.

The Philharmonic's Friday afternoon audience is among the most dignified and restrained concert groups known to music. The ladies—for that audience is mostly composed of ladies—usually pat their fingers together politely when something pleases them or just plain sit on their hands when it doesn't. Invariably, a large number start streaming out sometime during the course of the last piece so as to avoid the rush. Every artist, every conductor grits his teeth in anticipation of the occasion, knowing that his most sterling performance will detain none but the relatively few and hardy music lovers.

Van was to play after intermission. I knew that he had won a tremendous ovation the night before, but that doesn't guarantee Friday's reception, and I went to see what would happen. I could hardly believe my eyes and ears. Scarcely anyone left before the end. At the last chord a screaming crowd rose as one with a paean of acclamation for Van, Leonard Bernstein, and the orchestra, with whom Van insisted on sharing the triumph. After bringing the artists out for eight curtain calls the audience walked out reluctantly, dabbing at damp eyes, visibly shaken. I heard one woman say in a choked voice, "I can't explain it, but it was so much more than a musical experience."

Backstage and winding down into the corridor, a snake-line formed, kept in control by Benny, the lions' stalwart gamekeeper. For over an hour Van signed programs, recordings, pictures, matchboxes, torn bits of paper, anything on which a name could be written. And, as usual, a word or several words for everyone. One woman said, "Mr. Cliburn, I've come twenty-five hundred miles from Utah to hear you and see you. I have two boys studying piano, and they made me come so I could tell them about you." Van looked helpless but only for a second. "What're their names?" he asked.

Borrowing some paper, he sat down and began to write them at length while dozens and dozens waited their turn.

The Saturday night performance was followed by a similar backstage mob scene. Then to the Rainbow Room at Radio City to a dinner dance given by the David Rockefellers. Van ate and sipped club soda and danced until 1 A.M., then took his leave. Everyone was certain he was headed straight for bed, in view of the final concert next day.

Not at all. With Kondrashin and a small group of friends he went home with Mrs. Leventritt. Heading immediately for one of the two grand pianos in the living room, he played the Prokofiev Third Concerto while Kondrashin waved his arms over the imaginary orchestra. After that they played the Brahms Second Concerto on the two pianos. The party broke up after three.

Next morning Van was at Riverside Church before eleven to hear a performance of his "Anthem," composed to the 123rd Psalm. After the services a spontaneous demonstration started inside and spilled out to the street where passersby joined in for a handshake.

Van had just enough time to gulp a bite and change his clothes before walking on the stage of Carnegie Hall that afternoon. A reception "to greet Van Cliburn" was scheduled uptown from five to seven. Benny bolted the stage doors, enabling the pianist to escape and to arrive promptly, looking white and weary. It was obvious that he had given his last morsel of energy and that it had been worth it, as attested by Leonard Bernstein's first remark when he had walked in five minutes before Van: "It was thrilling to conduct for our boy today. He was fabulous, really fabulous."

When, at the party, Van saw many of his closest friends, the dining-room table full of food he liked, and a whole case

of Seven-Up, he revived in a flash, bounced right back to
entertain and be entertained. At eight o'clock he was off to
catch a plane for the next town, the next tornado.

Whether or not he is with you, you cannot escape him.
After the party we went to a mid-town restaurant. We had
hardly sat down before the maître d'hôtel told me that ever
since Van had dined there—once, months before—they'd developed an entirely new clientele. Every day teen-age girls
come in and immediately ask, "Where did Van Cliburn sit?"
If the table is occupied they wait for it patiently, no matter
how many other tables become available. Others phone for
reservations: "I want Van Cliburn's table."

I have yet to walk into a record shop without being informed for the umpteenth time that no previous classical
record has ever been bought by so many teen-agers as Van's
Tchaikovsky disc. Friends of ours recently discovered the
cause of the interminable length of their children's phone
calls: they play Van's record to each other.

But this devotional following is not confined to youngsters. Nor even to the United States. A few months after
Van's return from Brussels, William Schuman made a tour
of Belgium, France, and Holland. Every record shop he
passed was plastered with Van's records, and in between the
records were pictures of Van. Not the kind that RCA Victor
sends along for publicity display, but pictures of Van bussing the proprietor or hugging members of the proprietor's
family.

Schuman told this at the Lotos Club State Dinner given
in Van's honor. The president of Juilliard whimsically went
on to credit Van with having ended the '58 "recession" singlehandedly. Cliburn's triumph and the ticker-tape parade
had stimulated newspaper circulation, he said. Lights were

being turned on in formerly empty auditoriums, ushers were back at work, cabs were inadequate to handle the crowds going to and fro, restaurants were jammed before and after Cliburn concerts. "And only this afternoon," he mused, "I was in a Westchester discount store, and as I walked in the loudspeaker filled the air with the day's bargain items: 'Foist-floor rear, a sale on garden foinature. Foist-floor front —for thuree dollaz and twenty-nyun cents—Van Cliboin's recording of the Consairto by Tick-cows-skee.'"

We howled. Van doubled up.

Charles and Lyde Devall, publishers of the *Kilgore News Herald*, were also at this Lotos Dinner, representing Mr. and Mrs. Cliburn. "Well, what do you think of your home product now?" I inquired, glancing around at some of the most eminent men and women in the nation.

"Biggest thing that ever happened to Texas," Mrs. Devall answered. "Used to be oil wells, now it's Van Cliburn." The whole state, they told me, was gearing itself up for Van Cliburn Day in Texas on December 2, and Kilgore was buzzing with plans. They plastered a huge likeness of Van right across the main drag, and Governor Price Daniel flew into town to keynote the speeches. Only once before had the state ever proclaimed a special day for a living Texan—for John Nance Garner on his ninetieth birthday. Van was given another key to the city, this time a gilt one as tall as himself, and a plaque was presented to him by the Chamber of Commerce. A proud moment for Mr. Cliburn came when he was chosen to pin a Rotary emblem on his son which signified Van's election to the organization as an honorary life member.

One of the most jubilant women in town was Frances Gertz, who has headed Kilgore music committees for years.

"I've spent my life being general chairman for Van's recitals and concerts," she said happily, "but really, this was the *greatest!*"

Also the "greatest," but in a less public and more restrained way, was the dinner Calvary Baptist Church had given for Van and his friends at the church, earlier in the fall. Miraculously, they had been able to keep the church from being mobbed and to hold down the list of guests to a mere two hundred. But at least for one evening Van was able to move again among many of his old-time associates, play for them, talk with them, and accept the fine and handy leather-bound Bible they had bought for him.

Van had been frankly enjoying all his popularity, all his acclaim, all the lionizing just about five months when he said to me over the phone: "You know, Abram, I am so grateful. I'm so thrilled. But I must admit things sometimes *do* weigh me down." I commiserated with him, saying that I had observed the pressures, the wire-pulling, the intrusions and interventions which necessarily disrupted his life and must certainly try his soul. He answered slowly: "I've appreciated this little—er-er—good fortune tremendously. But I know how ephemeral fortune is, and believe me, if it all just folded up tomorrow and I had to go back to Texas to teach and practice, honestly, Abram, it wouldn't hurt a bit."

I had no doubt of his sincerity, though I realized that he was unusually fatigued at the time. Nevertheless, despite Van's inability to recoup entirely from his strenuous schedule, he has canceled few performances because of his own ill health. He did promptly postpone several recitals, however, when his mother developed an agonizing facial neuralgia which necessitated her being hospitalized in Dallas. Alerted to the possibility of an operation, Van dropped everything and flew to her side. As soon as she was able to travel he brought her up to New York for attention.

It was at this time that Van came to WQXR to hear tapes of the Rachmaninoff Third we had made during the broadcast from Carnegie. I thought he might consider it as a possible recording release, for in my opinion it was his finest performance of the work.

He arrived for our nine o'clock appointment bearing a small brown paper bag. Apologizing for being a little late, he explained that he had taken his mother to the doctor. In the tape room he opened the bag and spread out two hamburgers on rolls and a container of black coffee. When it comes to hamburgers Van says he's like Wimpy in the funnies. While we were listening Van said, "It really went better in Boston, Abram. You know, I've learned so much about this piece since May."

In the middle of it Royal Marks, Van's personal representative, walked in the door with Mrs. Cliburn. She was the picture of pain, and her son was so distressed to see her obvious suffering that he jumped up, overturning the half-filled container of coffee. He had been too immersed in the music to do more than merely nibble at his "supper."

We settled Mother into a chair where she sat in complete silence throughout the playing, her eyes closed, her face a combination of physical misery and emotional pleasure. As Van sat there he would say, "Oh no!" over something he didn't like; or at passages that pleased him, "Oh, marvelous . . . *just* what I wanted——" Then half apologetically to Martin Bookspan, WQXR director of recorded music who was officiating at the tape machine: "You know, I'm usually not *crazy* about my own playing."

After the session I inquired about Papa Cliburn. Van

said, "I spoke to him on the telephone last night. After reporting Mother's condition, telling him it's as good as can be expected, he said that he'd probably go to a company meeting in New Orleans. I said, 'Daddy, just take care of your health.' It's a record we keep playing to each other. You know—do as I say, not as I do."

It was near midnight. I drove Mother Cliburn to Van's apartment, while he and Marks were off to his eleven o'clock appointment with executives of RCA Victor. I never did find out when that meeting broke up.

In human experience Van Cliburn has lived a brimful lifetime in one year. It has been a sobering experience. He speaks and acts not with the air of a wonder boy with the world before him, but with the feverishness of one whose time is running out. And within his mind lurk the same questions that lurk within ours. Where can one go from a peak? Where can Van Cliburn go from here?

Obviously, he cannot play much more or earn much more than he does now. His problem is to develop further as an artist and as a man, and this is indescribably difficult in the climate of celebrity which allows too little time for work and contemplation and too much adulation for self-perspective. Cliburn is in an unenviable spot and must be given every chance to work out his future. Whoever isn't willing to give it to him is as vulnerable to criticism as the uncritical worshipers who see him and everything he does as flawless.

"The time must come," he told me, "when I must do everything I want to do." This statement, from a musician to a musician, represents the desire to express everything that lies deepest in art and in life. To achieve this goal he will have to do what all other sterling artists have done—withdraw from the spotlight periodically to enrich his mind and spirit and to nourish his heart and vision.

But he must also avail himself—not for too long—of his present chance to gain a solid professional eminence and the financial security that can provide eventual opportunities for unharassed development. We must never lose sight of the fact that the day Cliburn walked onto that Moscow-bound flight he was a twenty-three-year-old keyboard genius who had won our top awards, impressive artistic recognition, many major engagements, and baskets of critical bouquets. Yet had he decided instead to walk across the stage of Carnegie Hall that day, his appearance would have stirred about as much excitement among ticket buyers as the appearance of William Faulkner at Stillman's Gym. And had Cliburn not been victorious, the chances are that he would face the same situation today.

No one knows this so well as Cliburn, and it has given him a keen sense of responsibility about the power of his decisions and actions to help or hinder the cause of his fellow American artists. He keeps proving it in remarkably altruistic ways for one so young. When he says, "This is a good thing to do," he does not necessarily mean good for Van. Over and over he keeps expressing the hope: "Maybe some of this will rub off on my colleagues."

There is heartening indication that some of it will. The 1958 Leventritt finals for string players were personally covered by Ross Parmenter, music editor of *The New York Times*, who devoted a three-column story to a comprehensive description of the event. Mr. Parmenter not only reviewed the performances and ran a picture of the winner, Arnold Steinhardt of Los Angeles, but also set down his detailed reactions to all of the six finalists.

Within the past six months the press coverage of the activities and achievements of our artists here and abroad has been markedly more extensive. The large and small foundations have been gratified to observe that a wisely administered institutional grant to an individual, rather than to an organization, produced so consequential a result.

At this writing, eight months after Moscow, the National Association of Concert Managers of the United States and Canada proposed at their annual meeting to probe the possibility of an arrangement with one or more established musical awards whereby proven young artists would win, not only the orchestral appearances now offered, but also a tour of some thirty solo engagements throughout the country.

William Judd of CAMI and other prominent managers have noted an entirely new public interest in music and a mounting emphasis on native performers. Schuyler Chapin declared, "American artists in the future will have more dates, better dates, bigger fees, and more respect as artists, because of Van Cliburn." And still other prophecies and omens are in the air.

Mr. Cliburn can take a bow. He has indeed won a new respect for his fellow artists at home and for Americans everywhere. But it was a close call, and the law of accident had to be invoked heavily. That is what we must be bright enough to avoid in the future.

On the very day that Mme. Lhevinne had left me with the thought, "Now we have to find the money to get him over there," I found myself at a dinner seated near a member of the White House Palace Guard. "When you find the time," I whispered, "I have an idea you might want to pass on to the President. I think it could write his name large in our cultural history." The gentleman's eyebrows exhibited interest. Actually, I had several ideas. I still have, though one of them is a bit late—the suggestion that the President find a few dollars of the taxpayers' money with which to invite five or six young soloists (including one Van Cliburn) who were available and brilliantly able to represent us at competitions abroad. It seemed to me that none of them could fail to win at least esteem and good will for themselves and for us. The time seemed propitious to reply to the political propaganda that portrays us as money-grubbing illiterates, to say nothing of the bolstering effect of governmental recognition on the morale of these youngsters. I never did get to submit my ideas. I did, however, acquire a collection of gracious notes on handsome White House stationery which gained me a new regard from my secretary. The contents are a set of variations on the theme, "I'm looking forward to our chat. We *must* get together when both of us have an hour."

Although it remained for the Soviets and their Ministry of Culture to teach us that an artistic achievement is a mighty achievement, the ensuing response to Cliburn's attainment from our highest echelons of municipal and federal governments may be a heartening sign of the American capacity to learn. Perhaps it may finally impress upon the official representatives of the mightiest democracy on earth the vital need for a long-delayed recognition and representation of our cultural life within government itself.

We have a Department of Agriculture. How about a Department of Culture? We have a Secretary of Commerce. Who's attending to our commerce in ideas? Perhaps some annual congressional scrolls and presidential awards wouldn't hurt either, to glamourize our artists and thinkers, our creators and interpreters, our poets and historians. An

Arts Council or a Federal Advisory Commission or what-have-you would help to demonstrate that those who are currently living a pretty rough existence in the pursuit of the true and the beautiful are important national resources, worthy of our serious concern.

In the long run it is people who matter. It is what people value that determines their attitudes and actions. We are being gradually educated in sufficient numbers now to constitute a selective and articulate group. Now it only remains for our people, our administration, and our legislators to take fire from one another to establish art as a mainstream of our national life.

If it's good, sturdy American sense and practicality we're after let's look at the record. Our artists and our scientists have made our most effective ambassadors, even in the most unyielding strongholds of political prejudice. They have set examples for all others to emulate.

Van Cliburn is the whetstone on which our nation has sharpened its artistic awareness. He has brought a vital issue squarely before millions who previously never gave it a thought. His is a great accomplishment. No classical dramatist could have contrived a more perfectly timed entrance than the one fate accorded him. And if this entrance was magnificent, so was the way he rose to it.

The Van Cliburn experience should go far to stir our pride, to strengthen our cultural climate, to fortify our confidence in our own judgment, and to eradicate at last the view of art as a peculiar phenomenon unrelated to everyday American life.

13

Pianist and Musician:
The Critical Appraisal

Cliburn's pianistic gifts, as we have seen, were always self-evident. From infancy, playing the piano was to him not only a way of life but also life itself, and there is no surer sign of the born performer.

The great irony of the Cliburn success is—that he deserves it. He is a superbly equipped instrumentalist who makes musicianly sense and holds poetic ideals. Without effort or egotism he owns the unanswerable power of communication, the magic to which the spontaneous heart of the public is as responsive as is that of the most penetrating expert.

In short, a fully armed young artist walked onto the platform of the Bolshoi Salle in Moscow. And, contrary to popular opinion, he rose to favor and fame there on his performances of important solo works by Bach, Mozart,

Chopin, and the American, Samuel Barber. I know exactly what they heard and why they responded as they did, for I have several times reconstructed in my mind Van's competition performances of these compositions and of two Beethoven sonatas, too. Despite his extreme youth at the time, despite the fact that his playing did not exhibit the ultimate in scholarship or stylistic understanding, the music came out with astonishing musical intensity and intelligibility. In these works, strengthened by years of intellectual and emotional growth, buttressed by experience, Van swept the Soviet field, conquering the musicians and public alike, long before they heard one note of the Tchaikovsky or Rachmaninoff concertos.

Yet, and quite understandably, the scintillating sound and splurge of the piano-with-orchestra works made the finals particularly exciting and newsworthy. Inevitably, their triumphant reception produced an avalanche of orchestral offers. Everywhere, the public demand to hear the "prize-winning" concertos virtually dictated the programs, and Cliburn played one or the other or both works solidly for the first six months of his newly found career. In addition, and at every performance, he acknowledged the persistent acclaim of his vast audiences with solo encores by Chopin, Brahms, Liszt, Rachmaninoff, and Ravel.

For me, perhaps Cliburn's most impressive achievement is his ability to keep the meaning, the expressive content of music in front of an audience. This preoccupation is the more effective and surprising because it is more normally the attribute and ideal of maturity. Though he is a marksman of exceptional accuracy with technique to burn, he refuses to attract undue attention to it. No pianist owns a lovelier natural tone or has more lyrical aims. In a showy repertoire calculated to wow the public, he avoids melodramatics in the blood-and-thunder passages and seeks subdued and subtle nuances in the melodic sections.

These are the final impressions I took away with me every time I heard the post-Moscow Cliburn, right from the first Carnegie Hall concert of May 19, 1958. I was hardly alone. The next day this concert fomented among the metropolitan New York press a burst of critical accord as rare as it was rapturous.

Louis Biancolli, the first to hail Cliburn at his Philharmonic debut, wrote in the *New York World-Telegram and Sun*:

> The occasion was truly memorable. The young man who seemed so stupendously gifted when I heard him four years ago has returned from his travels a mature and dazzling artist. . . . It was evident that a musical personality of extraordinary power had gripped the imagination of the crowd . . . He exceeded all expectations, high as they were . . .

Ross Parmenter, music editor of *The New York Times* concurred:

> Van Cliburn faced a major test last night at Carnegie Hall . . . of manner, of musicianship, of technical skill, of temperament and of interpretative insight . . . The applause that went up from the capacity audience showed that he had got over his great hurdle . . . The pianist lived up to expectations, something that hardly seemed possible after so great a build-up.

Wrote Harriet Johnson of the *New York Post*:

> The 23-year-old Texan demonstrated last night that a

stupendous virtuosity and grandeur of style are among us, youth included . . . The glamour, excitement and success were shared by Cliburn with 43-year-old guest conductor Kiril P. Kondrashin, the first maestro from the Soviet Union to lead an orchestra here. . . . [Cliburn] spoke to the heart, and the listeners, numbering almost 3000, responded with uninhibited enthusiasm.

Miles Kastendieck of the *New York Journal-American* sang in unison with his colleagues:

Van Cliburn plays in the grand manner as well as with a kind of breathless virtuosity. . . . It is no wonder that the Russians found his Tchaikovsky so captivating.

But unanimity is not life. Here and there dissension arose, not about the pianist, but occasionally about the musician or the music he played. Even in Russia, where, from this distance, it appeared that only unqualified praise greeted his art, the *Sovetskaya Kultura* corrected this impression the day after Van left. Although a news story paid him a final tribute, "Cliburn will probably write out the most vivid pages in the history of musical performances of our time," a critical appraisal in the same issue stated:

Cliburn is by no means a mature artist and often is uneven. But his phenomenal talent and dramatic approach to what others consider ordinary passages of music are what endear him to Moscow audiences.

In the *New York Herald Tribune* even Paul Henry Lang, who regards the music of Tchaikovsky and Rachmaninoff somewhat as Bernard Shaw regarded a cut of sirloin, still had highly complimentary words for the executant:

Mr. Cliburn delighted the audience with the kind of virtuosity that we associate with the grand pianists of a bygone age. . . . He is undoubtedly a pianist with extraordinary talent and genuine attachment to his art.

In evaluating Cliburn's repertoire Mr. Lang had other things to say. The following excerpt is a gentle augury of later and harder things to come:

Many of us regretted that so much ability should be wasted on such music. . . . What this gifted young man needs now is a more catholic study of music—not pianism, of which he needs little—and that with modern teachers. He must also realize that what he is now being asked to do is a sure way to permanent intellectual disability.

This point of view was at first disputed by Winthrop Sargeant in *The New Yorker*:

The Russians, it turned out, had been quite right. The long, weedy-looking twenty-three-year-old Texan with the furiously tomentose scalp and the fingers resembling stalks of asparagus actually proved to be a pianist in the grand manner. . . . The works Mr. Cliburn chose for the occasion were the Tchaikovsky Piano Concerto and the Third Piano Concerto of Rachmaninoff—and he played the latter, by the way, in its original version, including those passages Rachmaninoff himself later deleted, on the ground that the composition was too difficult for most pianists to tackle. It is now fashionable in some circles—notably those inhabited by composers incapable of writing effective piano music, who today constitute a majority—to disparage these celebrated works as mere showpieces. They seem that way, however, only when played by a mediocre pianist. Actually, they represent a complete command of the instrument and a deep understanding of the psychological purposes of pianistic artistry—qualities that are practically extinct in contemporary music. Mr. Cliburn's performances of the two concertos gave them all their inherent dignity, fire, and romantic tenderness, and in listening to him one realized anew what eloquent works they are, and why during their period the piano ranked as the most expressive of musical instruments. There are, of course, on the current horizon a number of pianists—one thinks of Artur Rubinstein and Louis Kentner, among others—who have a commendable grasp of the tradition embodied in these and similar works, and some of whom, owing to greater maturity, play them with even more finesse and suavity than Mr. Cliburn. Still, in all my years of listening to pianists I cannot remember a youthful artist who seemed to comprehend the traditions as well, or to give comparable promise of becoming a great virtuoso.

After performing the Tchaikovsky and Rachmaninoff concertos in Philadelphia, Washington, and again in New York, Cliburn took them and his parents abroad to make four debuts—in London, Paris, Amsterdam, and Brussels. The European press and public echoed the Russian and American enthusiasm.

Dr. Ellen Ballon, the noted Canadian pianist and educator, who was in London when Van appeared, described the event to me:

I went, as many did, not knowing quite what to expect. The Tchaikovsky was fine, but I was not so overwhelmed as one somehow demands from an artist who has caused such a furor. I did notice, however, his unusually lyrical approach and fine nuance, in spite of the impossible acoustics of that monster, Albert Hall, jammed to the roof with the Lord-only-knows how many thousands. Then Cliburn played the Rachmaninoff. After the first movement, I turned to my companion and I said, "In case you brought me here to verify any of your political suspicions, I regret to inform you that this young man is a great pianist and that we are hearing one of the greatest performances of this concerto we are ever likely to hear." I wanted to congratulate him, but I simply couldn't get backstage. Never have you seen such a solid phalanx of autograph hunters and photographers bear down upon one man. And for a pianist, not a prizefighter, *par miracle!*

Dr. Ballon was referring obliquely to an incident involving Rachmaninoff, who never told it without getting hysterical with laughter. He once sailed from England on the *Berengaria*. On boarding he noticed a horde of newspapermen and photographers. The aloof Rachmaninoff steeled himself against the inevitable, only to see them whiz right past him. Stunned, he wheeled around to discover that their quarry was Primo Carnera.

Cliburn's long association with the Tchaikovsky Concerto made it inevitable that this would be his first recording. It elicited high praise from most quarters and set off fireworks in others. Harold C. Schonberg, among the most perceptive and exacting piano critics of the daily press, wrote in *The New York Times* (July 6, 1958):

In his appearances last May and in his new Victor recording of the Tchaikovsky with an orchestra conducted by Kiril Kondrashin, Cliburn stands revealed as a pianist whose potentialities have fused into a combination of uncommon virtuosity and musicianship.

Schonberg then compares the current Cliburn to the promising talent of 1954 who performed the same concerto with the New York Philharmonic.

What a difference four years have made! Where Cliburn's tone was then percussive it is now full, resonant and capable of all kinds of nuance. This in itself is a major triumph, and in this reviewer's experience, unprecedented.

A well-known noncomformist among critics used the occasion not only to laud Cliburn but to smite two fellow critics. B. H. Haggin told the readers of the *New Republic* (August 18):

Paul Henry Lang's admonitions to Van Cliburn—in the *New York Herald Tribune* after Cliburn's concert —to forswear the path of flashy virtuosity—seemed to make sense about the pianist about whom one knew only that he had wowed the Moscow public with Tchaikovsky and Rachmaninoff Concertos. But one discovers that they make no sense about the pianist who plays the Tchaikovsky Concerto on Victor and whom Lang heard play it in Carnegie Hall. For it turns out that Cliburn is, certainly, playing an inferior work of Tchaikovsky that has become a virtuoso display piece, but that the operation is—like Toscanini's performance of the Dance of the Hours—strictly that of a musician playing a piece of music and employing for the purpose not only a remarkable technical equipment but an equally remarkable and distinguished musical perception and taste. And one might add that the performance is that of the pianist who . . . needs no admonitions to forswear the path of flashy virtuosity . . . No less wide of the mark is Winthrop Sargeant's description of Cliburn, in *The New Yorker*, as

. . . a living representative of the great 19th and early 20th Century school of virtuosity, which included such formidable artists as Sergei Rachmaninoff, Josef Lhevinne, and Josef Hofmann, and it is indeed heartening to find the traditions flourishing again in one so young.

. . . Sargeant refers correctly to Cliburn's "tasteful and assured use of rubato," but then adds "in the style of the distinguished virtuosos of the past," which is incorrect; what distinguished Cliburn from those virtuosos is precisely his tasteful use of the rubato which they used tastelessly.

Irving Kolodin's reserved reaction in the *Saturday Review* (July 26) revealed some interesting, behind-the-scenes information about the recording sessions:

So much has been written (and read) about Van Cliburn in recent weeks that there is hardly anyone who doesn't have a position on the subject. Mine is that this recording is not as good a performance of the Tchaikovsky concerto as the Carnegie Hall one on his return from Moscow, that it nevertheless testifies to his exceptional power as a pianist though it is a less than first class recording, especially where the piano itself is (crucially) concerned.

Considering the stresses and strains to which Cliburn was subject in his frenzied activities in Russia and America prior to this recording, it would have seemed rather more desirable to process the performance itself as a documentation of that event, whether it was technically perfect or not. Instead, a session was arranged (at Manhattan Center) for a morning following his trips to Philadelphia and Washington. The pianist was so spent that it had to be abandoned. Carnegie Hall was engaged for the following midnight, and this is the outcome.

It doesn't strike me as possessing either the zest or the vitality Cliburn commanded on May 19, although this may be a reaction, after second hearing, to some localized ideas of tempo held by Kondrashin. On the whole, these tend to be slower than those to which we are accustomed, especially the opening pages, and two interludes later in the first movement. I am more at variance with his interpretation of "tranquillo" and "poco piu lento" at two other points in the first movement, for each interferes seriously with the momentum of the performance. The feeling persists that Cliburn is trying to pull him ahead, without succeeding.

Throughout—and with more ensemble success in movements two and three—there are ample evidences to support the high praise Cliburn has won as a pianist (as distinguished from an interpreter). Save where the jangly pick-up of his instrument tends to blur the sound, he is in majestic command of the work and its technical difficulties from first to last, with more than a few moments of subtlety.

The reactions of the musical press were of interest, as always, to the intellectual fringe. But no review or collection of reviews, no matter what the tone, had any power to affect the public demand for this disc. Its unprecedented success quite naturally led RCA Victor to hope for others from Cliburn. At this writing the hope has not yet materialized, despite the existence of several tapes of the Rachmaninoff and Schumann concertos and of solos reproduced from concerts and recording sessions. The answer lies in Cliburn's attitude toward his recordings: "I would like to scrap them," he said. "They aren't true because they report one isolated moment."

More to his satisfaction, evidently, were the personal successes he was chalking up in the outdoor concert stadia throughout the country directly after his lone recording was issued. The impression he made in the Midwest was summarized in the *Chicago Tribune* of July 17 by Claudia Cassidy, whose piercing pen has kept many a performer a safe distance from the city whose appellation "windy" carries for them an especially ominous connotation:

> It takes stellar stuff to come thru when the chips are down. Van Cliburn came thru. Making his Chicago debut Wednesday night with the Grant Park Symphony Orchestra, Mr. Cliburn stepped out with the front rank runners. I don't mean anything so absurd as to say that his career is made on two concertos. I mean that pianists run in the front rank or they don't run at all. Mr. Cliburn runs. In fact, he races like a thorobred.
>
> There just is no other way to play Rachmaninoff's Third Concerto, the great showpiece in D minor, which sounds magnificent when it is right, trashy when it is wrong. In my time I have heard three men play that

Third Concerto to set the stars spinning. They were Rachmaninoff himself, Horowitz, and Kapell. If he did not always set those same stars spinning, Cliburn reached for them, touched them, and sometimes, magnificently, they sang . . . This was big, brilliant, beautiful playing. Playing in the grand manner, with sweep and fire and style. Playing with bravura and the bite of the highly charged phrase turned at the point of impact. Playing rich in the liquid embroideries of the score, glittering in its love of spectacle. And something more, too. Even now, the imprint of something personal. Something of which you can say with conviction, "That's Cliburn." It's a big talent. In the hullabaloo of sensation, wish him well.

Three days later, in the *Chicago American*, Roger Dettmer pointed out a faction which wished Van anything but well:

> One cannot envy Cliburn his new-won celebrity . . . snipers have climbed into trees wherever he plays, their sidearms oiled and their trigger-fingers itchy. A whole crowd of the musically aware (that, I think, is their self-description) so resent his success . . . that they scarcely can contain themselves waiting for some, for any misstep.
>
> Mr. Cliburn, by winning the Moscow competition (let's face it, at this moment the most exotic place to win anything except stoning), has eclipsed the world's younger artists. . . . It has been darkly intimated by not a few that the whole business was "arranged" by the Russians for propaganda. . . .
>
> And so, even granting political chicanery? The point

was, is and will go on being, always primarily, that Cliburn is possessed of such talent that he earned his prize, Soviet motives be damned.

He can't anywhere now, afford to play a Beethoven sonata promisingly only; he must play it masterfully or postpone its performance until he feels it is masterful. That is the price of Van Cliburn's success in a society that lives by imbalance.

The sum of Cliburn's impress in two appearances on the West Coast was computed by Albert Goldberg in the *Los Angeles Times*. On July 31 he was commending but cautious:

> One year ago, had Van Cliburn been announced as a Hollywood Bowl soloist, the regular subscribers and a small group of cognoscenti would have heard him—if anyone had had the foresight to engage him, which is doubtful.
>
> Last night . . . the young Texan pianist played to an assemblage that filled the vast acreage of the Bowl to its last seat at a special concert at advanced prices. . . .
>
> On the whole one would say that Mr. Cliburn is deserving of all the acclaim. Tchaikovsky's B flat minor Concerto, which he played with the Los Angeles Philharmonic Orchestra under the direction of Thor Johnson, does not tell all that one would like to know about any pianist, but it tells enough to put this particular performance in the championship class. . . .
>
> His approach to the Tchaikovsky Concerto was in many respects unorthodox. It was basically slower and more deliberate than recent tradition has prescribed . . . it was thoughtful and it was often very beautiful.

. . . It was also something of a piecemeal conception, in which the details did not always fit into a strongly cohesive, over-all pattern. But this is something which is inherent in the artist's youth, and which time and experience will probably bring him to view differently. . . .

The next day Mr. Goldberg went overboard:

For the first time in history an American pianist filled Hollywood Bowl to capacity on two consecutive nights. It was a stirring occasion and if Van Cliburn has become a hero to his fellow countrymen one can honestly say on the strength of his playing of the Rachmaninoff D minor Concerto . . . that he fully merits all the adulation. This was a magnificent performance. . . . Only Horowitz has matched the limpid tone with which Cliburn set forth the opening theme. . . .

The Rachmaninoff and Tchaikovsky Concertos still have not told everything one would like to know about Mr. Cliburn's art. A full estimate will have to be reserved until one hears him play Bach, Beethoven, Mozart and Chopin in recital. . . .

On August 4, Cliburn was back in New York to repeat his spectacular triumph, this time at the Lewisohn Stadium. Ross Parmenter's review in *The New York Times* dispelled any suspicions that by this time the artist could hardly help being assailed by ennui:

What was also remarkable—in view of the month that Mr. Cliburn has been barnstorming with these same two concertos—was that he also gave them interpretations that were still magnificently fresh, still meticulous in their musicianship, and still marked by a degree of poetic inwardness that one would think difficult to maintain after so many appearances. . . .

Jay Harrison said in the *New York Herald Tribune* that it was not remembered when so many people, unable to find seats, sat down on the grass of the stadium or were engaged in such scurrying around to find places to sit. Calling it both "Van Cliburn night" and "pandemonium night," Mr. Harrison commented that the pianist, "because he chooses to play music which alternately bursts with vitality and caresses with poetry, is able to roar and whisper depending on the demands of the occasion. In all, there was lightning in his work. It illuminated his pieces to their marrow."

Cliburn went abroad again on August 14 to fulfill his promise made to officials of the Tchaikovsky Competition that he would appear as soloist with a Soviet orchestra at the Brussels Fair. The trip had no further artistic significance apart from another gesture of largess and another debut—a recital appearance for the U. S. Seventh Army in Heidelberg.

Returning about a month before the concert season was to open, Cliburn planned to prepare his recital repertoire and certain concertos he had resolved to play, notably the Brahms Second, Prokofiev Third, Mozart, K. 503, Liszt E-flat, and the Schumann. He had played most of them before but infrequently and years ago. It was his hope to work undisturbed, to have chances to try things out in relatively unexposed spots. Neither materialized, as we know, due to circumstances beyond his control.

One thing was always clear to Van, right through the tumult and the shouting: in order to fulfill himself, in order to fulfill the clamorous demand for his appearance, he would have to overhaul the works he already had studied and build a large new repertoire, especially for the cities which were to hear him several times.

The thing that was not clear to him was—how to effect it. In the blinding bliss of his initial conquest Van envisioned an artistic life that would enable him to call all his shots. He imagined an orderly regime which would permit tranquil periods of preparation. He assumed that engagements could be controlled to progress from smaller to larger centers, allowing him to take what Vladimir Horowitz calls "the first cold baths" in comparative privacy. He conceived not only work periods but also rest periods, prolonged enough for self-scrutiny, for reading, for a good hard look around. The cataclysmic forces of public ownership, of private afflictions and responsibilities shattered the chimera.

Came fall. The New York Philharmonic announced that Van Cliburn would play two concertos at each of his four October appearances, a coupling of the Mozart and the Prokofiev. A later announcement contradicted this. Cliburn would play—the Rachmaninoff Third at all the concerts. Murmurs and questions began to fill the air, this time from laymen as well as from professionals.

I first got wind of the impending critical reactions over the telephone from critic Kolodin, who is also the Philharmonic program-annotator. "I just got definite word," he said morosely, "that Cliburn is playing Rach Three. Isn't there *anyone* to give the young man advice, or won't he take it? Counting his first Carnegie concerts, plus the Stadium, plus the Philharmonics, he will have played it in seven consecutive appearances here. That won't do him much good, no matter how he plays it. I don't care about the Prokofiev; that's just more of same. But his intention to play a Mozart concerto couldn't have been better. He should've stuck to it."

At that time I hadn't seen or heard from Van in weeks, so I did not know the details of the altered decision. I only knew that he had submitted the Schumann Concerto and that the Philharmonic had to reject it because Eugene Istomin had long been engaged to play it the following week. Cliburn was terribly disappointed, because this was the one concerto he had chances to perform before his Philharmonic dates, in New Haven and in Boston.

I decided to find out for myself what had happened. Easier said than done. Telephoning him was almost useless: messages evidently never reached him. I sent a telegram. Four days later Van finally phoned. It was 1 P.M. He'd come "right down" if I was free for lunch. I was. An hour later he phoned to say he had been "hung up" and was starting out immediately. We sat down to eat and talk at 3:15. He looked awful.

"I didn't want to worry anybody," he said, "but I've been spending hours every day at the dentist's and the doctor's, meantime fighting for the strength and time to practice." I felt sorry but plunged right into what was uppermost in my mind. Why the Rachmaninoff again?

"You know about the Schumann," he said. "Next I thought of playing the Brahms Second and the Prokofiev Third. Over the phone Bernstein told me the Brahms wouldn't fit his program, so I asked, how about a Mozart concerto with the Prokofiev, and he said 'fine.' Then came the darned teeth and carbuncles and realization that I couldn't try out anything. When I remembered about the Philharmonic coast-to-coast broadcast and that I'd only been heard in the Rachmaninoff where I'd actually played it, that decided me. And after all," he concluded, "when I was originally engaged by the Philharmonic for one date it was for the Rachmaninoff."

I then told him candidly that he must be prepared for adverse criticism. "Critics can't be expected to take into account personal difficulties," I told him. "Their business is to judge artistic results."

Pushing his plate away from him, he leaned over and said, "I would rather have the critics say that I shouldn't have repeated the Rachmaninoff than say I was unable to play another concerto comparably well. I wouldn't dare to appear before the New York public and critics in a great piece of music which I felt needed more work, more experience. New York is no place for experiments.

"And," he continued, measuring his words carefully, "I can't see why anyone at this moment would want to push me into premature performances. Shouldn't they respect my respect for the music I play? I need more time to do justice to it and to myself; time I haven't had, and chances for tryouts I hoped to get and just didn't. I'm slaving on the Schumann and stealing every moment to get at the Mozart and Brahms. Why jump on *me*? There are artists who've been before the public twenty, thirty, forty years, who play the same two or three concertos season after season and never get criticized for it."

Although he expressed these sentiments with supernormal intensity he nevertheless went ahead and scheduled the Schumann Concerto for two pension-fund concerts with the Boston Symphony under Charles Munch. The event extracted a perceptive observation from Harold Rogers in the *Christian Science Monitor* of October 6:

You may call it many things—inspiration, poetry, heart, or spirit—but the little word that says more than all is love. This young man has a great capacity for loving—the music, the conductor, the orchestra, and his public. And there is nothing sweetly sentimental in this love. It is deep, serene, and secure. It is the quality that turns a good musician into a great one.

Who could fail to feel it at his performance yesterday afternoon? What else could inspire these simple though eloquent phrases in the Schumann A minor? What else could give him the magnificence of power in the climaxes, or these ineffable moments of tenderness in the pianissimos?

Cliburn's performance did abound in love and in many endearing things that stem from love. But I also observed faith in even greater abundance—the faith that a love of the music would by itself yield an organic conception and a fastidious command, the faith that what the heart feels the mind and hands will accomplish autonomically. This puts too large a burden upon faith. A firmer grasp of his subject matter, the sheer bedrock of repeated experience, was what Cliburn needed to match his work elsewhere.

The pianist evidently came to the same conclusion, judging from his reactions to the tapes when he, his mother, and I heard them later. From where I sat he had more criticism than love for the interpretation. At the very opening solo he threw up his hands exclaiming "Ach!" Several times, just before a section which had dissatisfied him at the original performance was about to come up, he turned to his mother and said, with a sardonic laugh, "Wait till you hear *this*."

It took me back to the time he had listened to various

tapes during his efforts to produce a satisfactory recording of the Tchaikovsky Concerto. When someone remarked that a certain passage was "full of intensity and daring," Cliburn shot back, "Yeah, and full of clinkers."

This is the Cliburn who instills confidence in his basic desire and eventual ability to accept fully his artistic responsibilities. His Boston appearance evoked recognition of these qualities from the exacting critic of the *Boston Globe*, Cyrus Durgin:

> Mr. Cliburn is an artist of no little stature. He plays with wholehearted devotion to the music at hand, with no display of ego or virtuosity. . . .
>
> The most important aspect just now is the way he integrates a solo part with the orchestra. You feel he is not giving a solo to accompaniment but is playing as a somewhat more emphasized instrument of the orchestra. That is a portion of the true essence of making music.

So it is. Yet this particular performance revealed to me not only Cliburn's truly great gifts but also the distance he must travel to crown them. Beyond doubt it substantiated his reluctance to accommodate those who insist that he play totally different works, and immediately. Another proof of his judgment was his subsequent rejection of a tape made later that evening in a recording session with Munch and the Boston Symphony. Cliburn recognized that the work was not quite ready for recording, in spite of the critical encomiums. "The greatest impediment to the maintenance of artistic balance," said Jascha Heifetz, "is the heady wine of continuous praise." Nowhere has Cliburn shown more evidence of artistic balance than in his refusals to put him-

self "on record" with performances he considered unrepr
sentative of his full musical intentions.

Continuous praise may come from compliant compa
ions and self-interested parties. But never, thank heaven
has it been the lot of any artist to receive it from the musica
press. When Cliburn played the Schumann in Dallas, Johi
Rosenfield wrote in the *Dallas Morning News:*

> The conquering hero returned Saturday night to the
> orchestra and the city that gave him its cheers much
> earlier. . . .
>
> After weeks of promise that Cliburn would essay his
> first Brahms B flat Concerto with Orchestra . . . the
> program was suddenly changed to substitute the Schu-
> mann A minor. It was announced that this was by
> "mutual agreement" of conductor [Paul Kletzki] and
> pianist.
>
> Rather obviously, neither Cliburn nor Kletzki had
> lived with it long enough—that is together—and the
> conveyance was neither as polished nor as accurate as
> the Rachmaninov . . .
>
> This is not to suggest that the Schumann was
> botched; it just wasn't ready for such an august oc-
> casion. . . .
>
> If the principals were hardly satisfied with either the
> work or the reception, their triumph actually came after
> the Rachmaninov Concerto. For then the crowd came
> to its feet and cheered lustily.

Great art is no accident, and Cliburn's youth makes it
hard to realize how many years he has studied, restudied,
and played over and over again the two concertos and the
solo works which catapulted him to fame. He must do no

less with other works, and many of them present profound problems. Cliburn recognizes this. But recognition is one thing; the knowledge to analyze accurately another; and the opportunity and apparatus to solve one's problems perhaps the most crucial of all matters relating to interpretative mastery. The way in which he handles these knotty matters, the degree to which he can resist pressure and learn from himself and from others—on these depend his ultimate artistic standards and achievements.

And precisely these were the primary considerations behind Cliburn's final decision to play the Rachmaninoff Third with the New York Philharmonic. Moreover, he simultaneously announced his intention of playing three "new" concertos for the Philharmonic Pension Fund in February 1959—the Mozart C major, K. 503, the Schumann, and the Prokofiev Third.

Shortly before the October appearances I met Kolodin one evening and passed on to him some of the things Cliburn had said to me on that subject. Kolodin sat silent for a few moments, then nodded thoughtfully and said, "Under the present circumstances—though I certainly don't subscribe to them—perhaps he made the right decision. We'll soon see and hear."

Kolodin not only saw and heard but wrote—in the *Saturday Review* of November 1—the first unfavorable criticism of Cliburn the interpreter to appear in the metropolitan press.

Separating all temporal facts from the enduring ones about Van Cliburn's reappearance in Carnegie Hall as soloist with the New York Philharmonic Orchestra under Leonard Bernstein's direction—such as whether he

should have played the Mozart and Prokofiev concerti originally announced for this date, and if he didn't, why he didn't—and reverting to a fundamental one, the question is: what kind of a performance of the Rachmaninoff No. 3 (for the thirty-fifth, thirty-sixth, thirty-seventh, and thirty-eighth time since his mission to Moscow) did he give?

For all its sweep and good musical impulse, a rather brittle-sounding, unduly melting, and in a certain sense feminine one. Time after time, a mental comparison with such available standards as the composer's own or the possibly more and certainly not less definitive statement of Vladimir Horowitz left one with the feeling that incisive attacks were being reduced to pin points of emphasis, while strongly affirmative statements of deep feeling were being downgraded to rather supine curves of sentimentality. A lack of tonal mass to override the orchestra at crucial points in the first and final movements was another limiting factor, plus an inclination to indulge the weaker aspects of the composer's creation at cost to the stronger. This is not to deny Cliburn the persuasion inherent in any musical point of view convincingly stated, and the audience reaction thereto.

The May 20 note of warning from Paul Henry Lang changed in pitch to disdain on October 18. In the *New York Herald Tribune* Dr. Lang asserted:

The second half of the program turned from earnest and respectable artistic endeavor to the opportunistic entertainment that characterizes much of our public musical life.

Van Cliburn, the young American musical gladiator who vanquished the heathen in Moscow, re-entered the arena only to run away from combat. The original program announced a Mozart concerto, than which there is no more revealing vehicle for artistic confession. But the clear, Mozartian consommé was withdrawn and Rachmaninoff, the borscht, restored to his "repertory." Thus once more we witnessed a re-enactment of the Battle of Moscow.

This just won't do. Everyone knows that he can play the Rachmaninoff very nicely, but the young man will have to make up his mind whether he wants to be an artist or a flesh and blood juke box which at the insertion of the proper coin always plays the same tune.

These are indeed relentless words. Yet the time comes when a critic, right or wrong, feels that he must speak his mind or fail in his duty to art, to the artist, and to himself. Some may feel that the time was not yet ripe; that within so short and hectic a period one could continue to give quarter with justification. But within the vitriol of Dr. Lang's review is a compliment: the finest critics will only summon their severest critical faculties in writing about the finest artists, those most worthy of their forthrightness.

Winthrop Sargeant, though still greatly impressed with the pianist, now began to share Dr. Lang's concern with the musician, and in *The New Yorker* of October 25 came up with a drastic suggestion:

> Along with a good many other people, I am beginning to be slightly worried about the sputnik-like career of Mr. Van Cliburn, which, it seems to me, may fizzle out unless it is based on a somewhat larger repertory

than he is playing at present. The problem is that he is so busy exploiting his rather phenomenal artistry in two or three concertos that he obviously hasn't the time to retire for a while and embark upon the study of the wide range of piano literature he must eventually master if he is to take a permanent place among the great pianists of our era. If I were in his place, I would withdraw from all concert activity for several years and return to painstaking study. But then this is Mr. Cliburn's affair, not mine, and I must say that his performance of Rachmaninoff's Third Piano Concerto at the Friday afternoon Philharmonic concert last week, under the baton of Leonard Bernstein, was, like his first here, a brilliant and altogether masterly one.

Withdraw for several years? At this moment? Only to find himself again at the starting post, this time in the even harder struggle to interest the fickle public in the achievements of a mature artist who was once a sensation?

No. I feel that this is asking too much. Apart from the fact that Cliburn is only now winning his public, his confidence in the future, and the economic security which, we hope, will enable him to indulge in periods of unhampered work, he also needs the practice of performance. Surely he must do much of his work in isolation. But no artist should work constantly in a vacuum. The processes of trial and error on the platform are essential to the performer's full development.

At this stage of his career Cliburn's time must be meticulously budgeted, his personal responsibilities reduced to a minimum, his repertoire carefully developed, and his concert commitments sagely apportioned. In my opinion, only in this way has he the chance to fulfill his phenomenal artistic potentialities without courting the virtual public anonymity he once experienced. Once he is solidly established, then, and only then, can he safely afford profitable but not overlong periods of absolute withdrawal.

A comprehending and sympathetic awareness of Cliburn's predicament was reflected in the tempered tone of Howard Taubman's review of October 18 in *The New York Times:*

> The Rachmaninoff Concerto, despite its sentimentalism, was another matter. Give credit to an exceptional performance by Mr. Cliburn and the orchestra. It is tempting to reprove the young pianist for begging off from the announced commitment to play something different and for returning to this concerto which, like the Tchaikovsky, has become his triumphal post-Moscow vehicle. But in the face of so enkindling a performance, one cannot complain.
>
> Mr. Cliburn traversed the concerto with dazzling freshness. The grand romantic manner, the big tone, the poetry were all there . . . Mr. Bernstein and Mr. Cliburn saw eye to eye on every detail and nuance of this performance. . . . Here was a memorable fusion of point of view and style.

The crucial test, a man alone with his piano, came in Richmond, Virginia. Cliburn's first recital here, since Moscow, instantly downed whatever skepticism existed in the Boston of the South.

Charles Scarborough saluted Cliburn in the *Richmond News Leader* of October 22:

Presented by Michaux Moody, the young pianist drew a full house despite some of the most disagreeable weather in recent concert-going history. . . .

The concert-goer in the United States is so accustomed to being offered a Russian, Polish, German, French or South American virtuoso that it is a source of pride to hear Van Cliburn of Kilgore, Texas, give a glittering performance of Liszt's "Mephisto Waltz" or the Chopin Scherzo in C sharp minor and that composer's Fantasy in F minor, as he did in Richmond last night.

But while those performances ranked with the best of the foreign or foreign-born virtuosi, it was not for technique alone that the Cliburn recital was notable. The 24-year-old pianist is disclosing an individual musical personality and a high standard of musicianship.

In a cruelly taxing program, Cliburn played three sonatas for the first section of his recital. They were Beethoven's "Appassionata," Op.57, the Mozart C Major (K.330) and Prokofiev's Sonata No.6. Many pianists would have contented themselves with this for a complete program. . . . Cliburn's Mozart . . . was neither sentimental nor condescending, but in the finest taste . . . played with a delicacy as striking as his power in other pieces.

John White's you-show-me attitude lends importance to the following excerpts from his review in the *Richmond Times-Dispatch*:

The phenomenal Texan who made a leap to world fame . . . showed Richmond how he did it . . . After an unusually generous program with three sonatas, assorted pieces, and two encores, he had his audience cheering. . . .

We were armed with plenty of critical reserve at the beginning, in spite of Cliburn's outstanding performances recorded and broadcast. The artist alone on the stage has a different kind of challenge—to make his playing big and small, sweet and fierce, to create music sufficient in itself and virtuosity that compels wonder, and to become in an hour or two an unforgettable personality. All of these things Van Cliburn did.

What was evident, if strange to some in the Prokofiev, became truly vivid in Chopin's C-sharp minor Scherzo and F minor Fantasy. The latter was the best performance we have ever heard. . . .

Van Cliburn has already and all at once a big, unique career. It is so thoroughly deserved that all of musical America will applaud him and hope for him. We will hope that nothing mars his natural development and ultimately great accomplishment.

Evidence that the pianist did not sit smugly on these plaudits is supplied within Marion K. Pinsdorf's review of the second recital in Englewood, New Jersey, written for the *Bergen Evening Record* of October 24:

The terrific pace being set by Cliburn . . . is evident. He said he was losing weight. An aide explained the pianist had practiced eight hours yesterday before the concert. Such practice schedules are planned at least four days a week.

On this encouraging note we conclude the general résumé of performances and critical reactions within the first six months of Cliburn's reborn career. His unsparing work in such a situation provides hope that he will not be deflected for too long by worldly exigencies. We can visualize him locked away with his piano for prolonged periods even as he tours widely and lives up repeatedly to the glittering reputation that precedes him, and everywhere leaving warm memories of his sunny spirit that responds naturally and liberally to the devouring demands from all sides for a fraction of his time.

His first breathing spell came during the uncommitted weeks of the 1958 Christmas holidays. Immediately he headed for California, specifically to spend many hours of many days in the genial and nourishing company of Bruno Walter. The desire for association with so profound a musician is verification that beneath the sensational surface of Cliburn's career flows the vigorous tide of serious aspiration.

There are other encouraging notes, among them one that is especially significant. Van Cliburn composes. Of all musical activities, composing requires the maximum grasp of musical materials. Right down the royal line of pianists— Mozart, Beethoven, Liszt, Anton Rubinstein, D'Albert, Busoni, Paderewski, Rachmaninoff, Schnabel, Hofmann, Horowitz—all composed. Hofmann once said, "I have yet to meet a supreme interpreter, with the one exception of Artur Rubinstein, who does not have considerable compositional talent, no matter how little it may be developed."

Cliburn occasionally plays as an encore a piece of his called "Nostalgia." Although he grows bashful when it is mentioned, I consider it excellent, as artful as its title is naïve, a far better piece than many an early opus by composers who later became celebrated. Ask him to play it sometime, and see if you don't agree.

He has written several other works, among them the "Anthem" on the text of the 123rd Psalm: "Unto thee lift I up mine eyes . . ." I heard an admirable performance of it at Riverside Church in New York one Sunday morning, given by vocal soloists Louise Natale and Doris Okerson, organist Frederick L. Swann, and a splendidly trained choir under W. Richard Weagly. The composition would do credit to any musical or religious program. It has the consistent warmth and dignity of Cliburn's personality and pianism and shows him to be a creative talent of no mean skill. His eyes light up in anticipation of a time when he can buckle down to some serious, concentrated composing and begin to evolve his own personal style. To musicians this is always an auspicious omen. And right now, he says, he has a piano concerto of his own "on the fire."

Obviously, a young man of twenty-four has a lot to acquire, a lot to crystallize, and a lot to examine. Interpretative maturity—the final ability to penetrate the entire substance of great music—can only be reached after a long and devotional quest. I have heard few artists in their twenties who could be said even to be launched upon the adventure, who ever articulate such an objective. Van is one who has, and it is another significant presage.

And I have yet to hear the artist at any age who could do everything equally well or wisely. The giants have always known this, and their final decisions followed years of soul-searching. As Cliburn probes deeper, as he gains insight he will find in art what he has told me he has found in life—that doubt lurks in the shadows of truth. Eventually, he will have to do what every sterling artist has done: retreat into reflection, make haste slowly.

No artist of stature was ever freed from these necessities

nor from the grueling labor of converting his new awareness into instrumental values. At the height of Rachmaninoff's mastery he was visited by Olin Downes, then the music critic of *The New York Times*. After admitting Downes, Rachmaninoff asked to be excused for a while. Sounds soon came to Downes from the next room—laborious repetitions of a section that evidently did not satisfy Rachmaninoff. It was from a Beethoven sonata for which the interpreter had long been famous. After a bit Rachmaninoff returned, sank into a chair, and stared dejectedly at the rug, heaving heavy sighs. "When and where does your tour start?" Downes ventured.

"Tomorrow, in Lynn," came the answer. "It will be r-r-rotten!"

The incident reflects the divine dissatisfaction which is the artist's armor. Van frequently shows signs of acquiring it, especially when he hears himself on tape and disc. At concerts I have several times gone backstage when he was still taking bows and playing encores. Despite the swarm of admirers around him, he has never failed to ask, "How was it?" When thunderous acclaim made hearing and speaking difficult, as at the Lewisohn Stadium when thousands stampeded to the stage, Van's raised eyebrows would frame the question.

His over-all standards have been so consistently high that I was always truthfully able to answer "fine" or to nod. But these are not moments for the whole truth and nothing but. They are moments of emotional need, when the artist asks for the assurance that professional opinion does not contradict public opinion.

But others ask questions and they expect straight answers. "If Cliburn's success is artistically authentic why didn't he have it before?" many have asked. I guess that it is hard for people who didn't know of Cliburn, who never knew the merciless facts of concert life in the United States, to believe that Cliburn did indeed have the considerable success described in these pages.

You see, in our country you can be the pianists' pianist, the musicians' musician, even the critics' delight—and all this can leave the mass public untouched. You can even have tremendous successes with individual audiences and still be where many of our finest artists are and where Van was—just about nowhere, because he had no public that was *his* public.

The music-loving skeptics ask specific questions in the effort to compare Cliburn with his American colleagues in his age group. Comparisons are usually misleading, because artistry is as unduplicable as people. But here, I think, an exchange typical of many I've had might serve some useful purpose.

"Is Cliburn a better musician than Seymour Lipkin or Jacob Lateiner?"

"No."

"Is he a better technician than Byron Janis or John Browning?"

"No."

"Has he more repertoire or a wider range of color and style than Gary Graffman or Leon Fleisher?"

"No."

"Has he more intellectual understanding than Eugene Istomin or Claude Frank?"

"No."

"Well, then, what gives?"

It's an excellent question, because something certainly has

to "give" besides quality for a musician to stand a ghost of a chance to survive in the merciless jungle of the concert business.

Every one of the artists just mentioned, and still other colleagues of Cliburn's, are performers and interpreters of the very first caliber. What "gives" with Van the musician is his emotional style, which has assuaged a public hunger for the Romantic Tradition, a nearly lost art and a blind spot for most of our twentieth-century players. An exceptionally rhapsodic ardor and communicative force set Van apart from the rest of his confreres.

But he had these qualities before Moscow, and they were duly acknowledged in the spoken and written opinion of a significant segment of the musical world of the United States. What finally "gave" to make them known to all is now history.

Nevertheless, Van was more than the right man in the right place at the right time. He was also the one who grasped the chance to stand forth as a living symbol of a current cause, the one who owned the greatest personal magnetism to sustain his role. By this I do not mean to detract one whit from Cliburn's artistic qualities or from those of his numerous colleagues who, each in his or her own way, are analogously equipped as pianists and musicians.

I am merely trying to fathom that indefinable power, given to the few, which goes into the making of an artist as well as into the making of a personality and a career. Artistic excellence alone is not always that which carries us out of ourselves, which stirs something profound and moving within us. That is a quality apart. Paderewski had it to a far greater degree than the pianistically superior Hofmann. Van has it, no doubt about that. Call it a humanized heart.

Call it what you will. It is as irresistible a force as the law of accident which provides or denies the other elements that enable it to shine forth.

Once the alchemy has been achieved, audiences await The Touch in sweet agonies of anticipation. Publicity can start it. Advertising can sustain it. But not for long. Meanwhile, some of it can become quite absurd. Arriving early for one of Van's Carnegie Hall concerts, I caught the conversation of two men sitting behind me:

"D'yuh feel it?"

"No, I don't feel nothin' yet."

"Well, you will. Like 'lectricity. Boy, that kid's dynamite!"

The orchestra assembled, the lights were dimmed, and the audience began to talk in excited little whispers.

"Feel it now?"

"No—not yet."

Another minute passed. All eyes were tensely trained on the platform.

"Feel it now?"

"Mmmm, sort of, yeah. I think I know what you mean."

When Van came out of the wings, both men suddenly jumped up, bellowing, beating their paws together madly, the Skeptical One trying to outshout and outclap his companion. Not a note had he heard. He didn't have to. He was already in a trance, carrying his magic within him.

The danger of mass adulation is not only its faithlessness, which shifts loyalties at the drop of a front page. It can also seduce the receiver, actually encourage him to adopt popular norms, to grow indifferent toward the highest standards, to grow satisfied with what can be "put over" rather than to aim at what he himself knows to be worthy.

This is the curse of the limelight at an early age. The extent of Van's celebrity and commitments make it all but impossible for him to learn the many things he needs to know. He is surrounded by audiences and associates who vie with one another in singing praises. Some who know enough and know him well enough to proffer advice have said nothing, knowing that at this moment he cannot stem the tide. Those who love him most—when they managed to get a moment alone with him—have spoken honestly, in the conviction and hope that at every opportunity he will take further counsel with himself and with masters such as Bruno Walter.

Far from Van's black-and-white ivoried tower, his colleagues put their heads together, troubled by aspects of his playing which they have not had the chance or the courage to discuss with him. They are bothered by his occasional unobservance of the text, by those efforts to attain expressive intensity when they sometimes lead to a loss of momentum or to playing so softly that the sound fails to penetrate; also by certain inconsistent phraseology in recurring statements and by insufficient concern for the rhythmic shape of themes and figurations which tend to break the coherence and continuity of large designs. Admittedly, these crucial matters are not yet firmly fixed in Cliburn's mind. And let's also admit, while we're at it, that there are plenty of fully established performers around in whom such matters are even less firmly fixed.

Considerable comment bears upon Cliburn's generally slower tempos. Nothing is more discussable or mercurial than the basic pace at which a piece should be played. A tempo that does not violate the essential spirit of a composition is a thoroughly workable premise, for tempo is no absolute. It is therefore not his basic pace that I would quarrel with, but its tendency, now and then, to ebb, even in spots where the composer asks for an accelerated speed. This does to music exactly what it does to speech, as when the word "nine" is subdivided to sound like "ni-en" in an over-leisurely dialect. Such things, however, have a charm of their own, are sometimes regional, and often derive from idiomatic influences. Mme. Lhevinne has observed that Van's pre-Moscow conception of the Tchaikovsky and Rachmaninoff concertos was somewhat brisker.

Finally, we might re-examine the matter of Cliburn's repertoire, for eventually everyone must face the music. A study of his solo inventory reveals it as unimpeachably catholic though somewhat circumscribed, for he used the same program throughout the first three seasons of his Community Concerts recital tours. Some other and significant works, however, appear on his non-Community programs. In this way Cliburn acquired a large platform experience with a repertoire that is undeniably more impressive in quality than in quantity.

It is not generally known that in Moscow he had listed, and was thoroughly prepared to play, the Handel-Brahms Variations, the Beethoven "Appassionata" Sonata, the Chopin B minor Sonata, and the Prokofiev Sixth Sonata, apart from the required works.

Additionally, Cliburn's concerto repertoire is far from negligible but has remained almost untried except for you-know-what. When he was among the young princes of Pianoland, Cliburn's repertoire was no source of worry. It appeared that he would have, more abundantly than he wanted or needed, the time and opportunity to study, probe, select and reject, and to experiment on and off the platform.

Then overnight he was enthroned, to find for himself how uneasy lies the head that wears a crown.

In response to all criticism of his repertoire, Cliburn has always quoted the musical epigram: "It's not what you play, but how you play it." It is a half-truth, no less and no more valid than the contrary contention that it is not how, but what one plays which matters. The truth lies somewhere between, and Cliburn's conviction is unassailable from the point of view that anything short of an authentic and comprehensive presentation of a masterwork renders it an ill-service.

Cliburn's development differed from that of pianists such as Godowsky, Schnabel, Hofmann, Rubinstein, Arrau, Bolet, Gieseking, and Serkin, who in their early twenties had an encyclopedic knowledge of the literature of their instrument. Godowsky, almost as famous for his intellect as for his artistry, was once asked: "How can you possibly learn so many works when you compose, teach, and travel so much?" He answered: "I don't learn them. I know them."

Let us assume for a moment that Cliburn had used the early years to learn and prepare adequately all the concertos of Mozart, Beethoven, and Brahms. How many would he be engaged to play? I recall the unsurpassed William Kapell telling me that his success with the Khatchaturian Concerto "typed" him for five solid years. Only then was he able to call some of his shots by playing the Rachmaninoff Second Concerto and the Paganini Variations. Not until the last years of his tragically brief span did he finally force the issue and introduce one Mozart and one Beethoven concerto into his orchestral itinerary.

I first ascribed this to Kapell's youth and lack of bargaining power, but learned better in a talk with Vladimir Horowitz, emperor of all he surveyed and entirely beyond such problems. Or so I assumed until he told me, "Year in and year out, all they want is the Tchaikovsky and Rachmaninoff. I have to fight to play Beethoven or Brahms, and often they fight back."

Cliburn had a taste of this when he announced that he would play the Schumann Concerto with a small-town orchestra, whereupon his management received an agonized appeal from an official of the organization. "Our subscribers are very disappointed," he said. "But if Cliburn won't play one of the prize winners, will you assure us that he'll play lots of encores?"

The complaints about Cliburn's "two concertos" arose mainly in New York, which had a bellyful of what the smart alecks dubbed "Ham and Eggs à la Russe" and "Tchai on Rachs" ("tchai" being an approximation of the Russian word for tea). Neither the complaints nor the gags were all maliciously meant: many were expressing in typical American fashion a genuine concern, a legitimate and heartening concern for Cliburn's future.

It is beyond my capacity to predict this future with certainty. I have merely attempted to present facts and opinions as fully as your patience permitted, and I have indicated my reasons for optimism, for believing that Van Cliburn is more than the sum of the parts. His special distinction lies not so much in his extraordinary pianism and musicianship, which from the highest standards are still understandably transitional, as in his dedicated attitude, his emotional freedom, and spiritual conviction. These are the rarities, precisely the qualities and forces so hard to find in our turbulent era.

Yet the very facts of this era have made a legend of him, and he must come to grips with the environment which has molded him and which he sees the chance to mold. At the moment, his technical equipment and his primary opportunities lie in the realm of music.

Our generation has seen classical music become more and more appreciated, available, and patronized. Nevertheless, the steadily increasing interest still reflected the taste of the musically discriminating. The mass public and its government continued in their insensibility and inaction toward art, artists, and their place in our society. The teen-agers were breaking up dance halls and movie houses in their delirium over the latest jazz fad. The statistics on juvenile delinquency were alarming.

Then Van came upon the scene, to become a national hero, a respected artist, and the newest idol of teen-agers: a man who opened the hearts of all and created for music a new public and a new climate. And upon the millions utterly deaf to his music or to any music, his achievements, his outgoing personality and earnestness of utterance have exerted an enigmatic power that has brought them a spellbinding interlacement of strength and cheer and belief. This, from a pianist, was something: something new on the face of the earth.

Naturally, Cliburn has become a sublimely confident and successful man. But what makes him certain to succeed in whatever he undertakes is also the pitfall. The Cliburn dilemma appears at the point where the self-contained artist's ambitions and the man's all-embracing ambitions conflict. Is it possible for him to reconcile his dilemma successfully? Eventually, perhaps, but not immediately. The core of the conflict is in the exacting demands of art and the sprawling demands of life. The standards today which enable a musician to attain and maintain the status of a master are too prodigious, too all-demanding. Soon Cliburn will come to the fork in the road. Soon he must choose.

The pianist is impelled in the direction of artistic fulfillment. He is being exhorted by colleagues and critics to play less or even to retire temporarily. At any rate, to study more and rest more, to make of himself the complete musician and supreme pianist he has it in him to become.

The man is impelled in still another direction which fits perfectly his human and religious ideals and promises a result possibly more significant to him than that of creating one more fine pianist. "The most glorious thing in life," he once said to me, "is not to do for ourselves but to pursue some image, some vision that we can bring about for others."

Playing the piano has been the public expression of Cliburn's faith in God, love for people, and vision of a better world. But it accounts only partially for his peculiar hold over masses of people in every walk of life. To them, his piano playing, remarkable as it is, is secondary to his position as one capable of mending political and spiritual afflictions of our time.

He knows this, and it has only added to the burden of decision. What should be his uppermost aim? To work for Cliburn the pianist or to work for a better society in which love and art, grace and peace shall abound? Perhaps both! The utopian ideal lives in many when they are young. Few in the world have ever had the opportunity to dream dreams for long or have ever attempted to convert them into reality without getting their heads bashed in. Who of us in our sophistication and skepticism has the right to deter anyone from fighting for a truth as he sees it? Especially one whose unique position promises some tangible outcome.

Actually, Cliburn is already launched on a conciliatory plan. He has thrown himself heart and soul into youth projects; he has committed himself to international tours which will undoubtedly yield immense good will all round. The artist is being engulfed for the moment while the man is fulfilling his vision and while the human being's swollen schedule is reducing him to a shadow. And through it all, he is working harder and doing more than any man I know —all of it with genuine altruism.

Even so, there is but one road to the pianistic Parnassus. Whether or not Cliburn undertakes the decisive ascent, whether he hews to the path and never looks back or falters —on these will depend the connotation and longevity of the Van Cliburn legend.

Fifty years from now when the name is evoked, what will it denote? Will it signify the name of a great musician or the name of a man, incidentally a musician, who was significant to the environment in which he moved? Or in twenty-five years will he have followed Albert Schweitzer's path to immolate himself entirely on the altar of service to mankind? Any or all of these paths would be rewarding—each in its own way—to him, to us, to posterity. From this vantage point none can say which is the optimum path. Each man who holds ideals must live his own way and find his own solutions.

As for a decade from now, Van Cliburn has supplied one answer himself, and characteristically:

"In ten years' time," he told his parents soon after his return from Moscow, "the Russians may not remember the name Van Cliburn. But they'll sure remember it was an American who won the first Tchaikovsky Competition."

We'll remember too. But only time will prove whether we'll remember it as a spectacular footnote to history or as a turning point in our cultural evolution.

Index

Index

Index

Index

Index

Index